RESURGENT RUSSIA:
AN OPERATIONAL APPROACH TO DETERRENCE

*A U.S. Army War College Integrated
Research Project in Support of:
U.S. European Command and
U.S. Army Europe*

R. Reed Anderson

Patrick J. Ellis

Antonio M. Paz

Kyle A. Reed

Lendy "Alamo" Renegar

John T. Vaughan

Foreword by Malcolm W. Nance

T0058185

Skyhorse Publishing

First Published by 2016 US Army War College Press.
First Skyhorse Publishing edition 2017.

Skyhorse Publishing books may be purchased in bulk at special discounts for sales promotion, corporate gifts, fund-raising, or educational purposes. Special editions can also be created to specifications. For details, contact the Special Sales Department, Skyhorse Publishing, 307 West 36th Street, 11th Floor, New York, NY 10018 or info@skyhorsepublishing.com.

Skyhorse® and Skyhorse Publishing® are registered trademarks of Skyhorse Publishing, Inc.®, a Delaware corporation.

Visit our website at www.skyhorsepublishing.com.

10 9 8 7 6 5 4 3 2 1

Library of Congress Cataloging-in-Publication Data is available on file.

Cover design by Rain Saukas

Print ISBN: 978-1-5107-2610-9
Ebook ISBN: 978-1-5107-2622-2

Printed in the United States of America

The United States Army War College

The United States Army War College educates and develops leaders for service at the strategic level while advancing knowledge in the global application of Landpower.

The purpose of the United States Army War College is to produce graduates who are skilled critical thinkers and complex problem solvers. Concurrently, it is our duty to the U.S. Army to also act as a "think factory" for commanders and civilian leaders at the strategic level worldwide and routinely engage in discourse and debate concerning the role of ground forces in achieving national security objectives.

The Strategic Studies Institute publishes national security and strategic research and analysis to influence policy debate and bridge the gap between military and academia.

The Center for Strategic Leadership contributes to the education of world class senior leaders, develops expert knowledge, and provides solutions to strategic Army issues affecting the national security community.

The Peacekeeping and Stability Operations Institute provides subject matter expertise, technical review, and writing expertise to agencies that develop stability operations concepts and doctrines.

The School of Strategic Landpower develops strategic leaders by providing a strong foundation of wisdom grounded in mastery of the profession of arms, and by serving as a crucible for educating future leaders in the analysis, evaluation, and refinement of professional expertise in war, strategy, operations, national security, resource management, and responsible command.

The U.S. Army Heritage and Education Center acquires, conserves, and exhibits historical materials for use to support the U.S. Army, educate an international audience, and honor Soldiers—past and present.

STRATEGIC STUDIES INSTITUTE

The Strategic Studies Institute (SSI) is part of the U.S. Army War College and is the strategic-level study agent for issues related to national security and military strategy with emphasis on geostrategic analysis.

The mission of SSI is to use independent analysis to conduct strategic studies that develop policy recommendations on:

- Strategy, planning, and policy for joint and combined employment of military forces;

- Regional strategic appraisals;

- The nature of land warfare;

- Matters affecting the Army's future;

- The concepts, philosophy, and theory of strategy; and,

- Other issues of importance to the leadership of the Army.

Studies produced by civilian and military analysts concern topics having strategic implications for the Army, the Department of Defense, and the larger national security community.

In addition to its studies, SSI publishes special reports on topics of special or immediate interest. These include edited proceedings of conferences and topically oriented roundtables, expanded trip reports, and quick-reaction responses to senior Army leaders.

The Institute provides a valuable analytical capability within the Army to address strategic and other issues in support of Army participation in national security policy formulation.

Strategic Studies Institute
and
U.S. Army War College Press

STRATEGIC LANDPOWER AND A RESURGENT RUSSIA: AN OPERATIONAL APPROACH TO DETERRENCE

A U.S. Army War College Integrated Research Project in Support of: U.S. European Command and U.S. Army Europe

R. Reed Anderson
Patrick J. Ellis
Antonio M. Paz
Kyle A. Reed
Lendy "Alamo" Renegar
John T. Vaughan

May 2016

The views expressed in this report are those of the authors and do not necessarily reflect the official policy or position of the Department of the Army, the Department of Defense, or the U.S. Government. Authors of Strategic Studies Institute (SSI) and U.S. Army War College (USAWC) Press publications enjoy full academic freedom, provided they do not disclose classified information, jeopardize operations security, or misrepresent official U.S. policy. Such academic freedom empowers them to offer new and sometimes controversial perspectives in the interest of furthering debate on key issues. This report is cleared for public release; distribution is unlimited.

*****

*****

Comments pertaining to this report are invited and should be forwarded to: Director, Strategic Studies Institute and U.S. Army War College Press, U.S. Army War College, 47 Ashburn Drive, Carlisle, PA 17013-5010.

*****

All Strategic Studies Institute (SSI) and U.S. Army War College (USAWC) Press publications may be downloaded free of charge from the SSI website. Hard copies of certain reports may also be obtained free of charge while supplies last by placing an order on the SSI website. Check the website for availability. SSI publications may be quoted or reprinted in part or in full with permission and appropriate credit given to the U.S. Army Strategic Studies Institute and U.S. Army War College Press, U.S. Army War College, Carlisle, PA. Contact SSI by visiting our website at the following address: *www.StrategicStudiesInstitute.army.mil.*

*****

The research team is indebted to many people for their incredible support and contributions to this project. First and foremost, the team is grateful to the project's sponsors, Lieutenant General Ben Hodges, Commander, U.S. Army Europe, and Mr. Michael Ryan, U.S. European Command (EUCOM) J9, for the time they dedicated to initial discussions that set the direction of the work. The team is further grateful for the time, candor, and insights provided during the many hours of research discussions with the aforementioned staffs and organizations. The team is particularly indebted to the staff and faculty of the U.S. Army War College and the Strategic Studies Institute who served as our mentors, guides, and critical eyes as we developed, drafted, and refined this monograph. Finally, and most important to any endeavor, we are grateful for the understanding and dedicated support of our families who sacrificed time with us in order to allow us to complete our work. Behind every good soldier, sailor, airman, and marine is an even better family. To them we dedicate our work.

CONTENTS

FOREWORD
BY MALCOLM W. NANCE

Change came rapidly and dramatically to the Russian Federation after the dissolution of the Soviet Union in 1991. A loss of national direction and purpose for many Russians came with the ideological collapse of communism. The following decade of painful transition brought with it a fledgling democracy, open borders, freedom of religion, and a massive influx of western products. Liberty and self-determination for the Russian people also brought massive corruption. Wholesale looting and cashiering of Soviet assets soon enveloped the country. Everything from entire regional electrical power grids, shipyards, airports, and military bases to supermarkets, farms, and shoe factories was sold, stolen, or misappropriated. The influx of billions in western investment led to an outflow of illicit cash and with it the feeling that Russia was becoming a failing mafia state.

The election of Vladimir Putin as president in 2000 brought about a financial, cultural, and historical realignment based on his promise of a resurgent Russian Federation determined to ascend to global leadership. Russian global power waned after the dissolution of the Soviet Union, and Putin openly rejected the framework of the United States and Europe and its expansion of the NATO security alliance into Eastern Europe. Under his leadership, Russia made strides in harnessing economic power through the sale of petrochemicals and weapons. The perceived strength of Vladimir Putin's autocratic rule has given Russia a slim advantage in reimagining the geopolitical sphere to its liking. This aggressive forward posture presents a challenge to identifying Russian Federation disruptive methods and actions that operate just below open hostility.

Vladimir Putin has set a path for a rising Russia that applies all dimensions of military, intelligence, and diplomatic power to achieve its strategic goals by disrupting geopolitical norms. Putin is attempting to rebalance the world by raising, encouraging, and quite possibly engineering the rise of autocratic regimes. If the American election of 2016 has taught politicians, diplomats, and intelligence analysts anything, it is that Russia will directly confront the role of NATO, push back the alliance's membership in Eastern Europe, and weaken the political and economic relationships between traditional American and western allies. Russian clandestine power has moved from the shadows to the forefront of their national power projection in order to protect their interests.

Putin's Russia has demonstrated capability to not only influence political events but to apply military and intelligence power to directly intervene in situations to its advantage. The 2014 Crimea crisis commenced with a series of covert intelligence actions, political propaganda, and cyberwarfare operations that culminated in an open armed invasion of the Ukraine to seize the Crimean peninsula.

Absent from the international conversation over how to confront the new Russian challenge has been the ability of the West to develop and prioritize a response at a level below open hostility to asymmetric challenges such as cyber-attack, propaganda, and other forms of hybrid warfare. The multifaceted deterrence approach offered within this volume is the most likely to be successful.

The United States consistently misinterprets Russia's goals and ambition to achieve them. This volume clearly reveals that the unforgivable error when dealing with Russia, particularly since their 2016 cyberwarfare attack on the American electorate, is that it must not be seen through the lens of western norms. Understanding Russia's culture and history and comprehending the Slavic experience that guides their decision-making are critical to any approach. This US Army War College study, *Resurgent Russia: An Operational Approach to Deterrence*, is one of the first doctrinal studies that identifies Russia's use of asymmetric political and propaganda warfare. It reveals that Russia manipulates the global information battlespace by injecting carefully crafted political and psychological warfare data into the global news and social media to achieve a national goal by which all others are balanced: information dominance.

Malcolm W. Nance is a career US Intelligence officer and a counterterrorism and national security analyst for MSNBC News. He is also author of The Plot to Hack America: How Putin's Cyberspies and Wikileaks Tried to Steal the 2016 Election.

FOREWORD

As noted in the *U.S. Army Operating Concept,*[1] senior leaders and planners face a very complex, unpredictable world. Witness for example, Russia entering the fight against the Islamic State, and then its subsequent alleged withdrawal of forces from Syria. Russia's actions certainly caught many by surprise—but should they have? Predicting Russia's actions is indeed challenging, and the task has been made more so since many Russian experts, linguists, and scholars have left government service in recent decades. This post-Cold War trend may be changing though, as Russian actions are becoming increasingly important to policymakers, strategists, and military leaders. Some leaders have gone as far as saying that Russia is the only existential threat to the United States—mostly due to its nuclear arsenal. Nevertheless, Russia's actions over the past few years have shown that the United States needs to devote greater attention to Russia, its intentions, and its leaders.

This monograph is one small—but important—step in that direction. In direct support of the U.S. European Command (EUCOM) and U.S. Army Europe (USAREUR), six U.S. Army War College students from the resident class of 2016 spent much of this past academic year investigating whether and how the U.S. Army is prepared to respond to various forms of aggression from Russia. Lieutenant General Ben Hodges, USAREUR Commander, Mr. Michael Ryan, EUCOM Director for Interagency Partnering, and their staffs in Wiesbaden and Stuttgart, Germany, gave generously of their time, and we are grateful to have had the opportunity to support them through scholarship. In conducting research in Washington, Brussels, Mons,

Stuttgart, and Wiesbaden, the student research team confirmed that, in fact, the United States has implemented a wide range of actions to counter Russia's actions. Yet their research brought to light questions over whether those actions are properly focused, particularly as it pertains to deterrence, as well as against a threat not entirely like that faced during the Cold War. This monograph seeks to flesh out the answer to these and other questions by exploring Russia's intentions, laying out a more modern approach to deterrence, and presenting recommendations and policy options for senior leaders within the Department of Defense (DoD) and across the interagency.

The Strategic Studies Institute (SSI) is pleased to publish this monograph. We are confident that the research, analysis, and recommendations expressed within will contribute importantly to the ongoing debate over national security and America's role in Europe.

DOUGLAS C. LOVELACE, JR.
Director
Strategic Studies Institute and
　　U.S. Army War College Press

ENDNOTES - FOREWORD

1. Department of the Army, U.S. Army Operating Concept, Win in a Complex World, TRADOC Pamphlet 525-3-1, Fort Eustis, VA: U.S. Department of the Army, October 31, 2014.

ABOUT THE AUTHORS

LIEUTENANT COLONEL (LTC) R. REED ANDERSON entered military service in 1987 as a U.S. Army Reserve combat medic and was commissioned in 1994 through the Reserve Officer Training Corps (ROTC) program at Brigham Young University as a Field Artillery officer. Following the artillery basic course, he spent two tours with the First Infantry Division in Kansas and Germany. Following battery command, LTC Anderson became a Europe foreign area officer, which has taken him on tours to Portugal, where he attended Portuguese Army and Joint Staff courses; the U.S. European Command; the U.S. Mission to the North Atlantic Treaty Organization (NATO); Afghanistan; and the Army staff. LTC Anderson holds a master's degree in international security affairs from the Naval Postgraduate School. His previous publications include several articles in the Foreign Area Officers Association professional journal, *International Affairs,* to include a series of three articles on the trans-Atlantic relationship, and a treatise on strategic and operational planning for theater security cooperation at the geographic combatant commands. LTC Anderson is currently a member of the U.S. Army War College resident class of 2016, upon completion of which he will serve as the Chief of the Office of Security Cooperation at the U.S. Embassy in Tunis, Tunisia.

COLONEL (COL) PATRICK J. ELLIS received his commission in the infantry upon graduation from the U.S. Military Academy in 1994. He served as a platoon leader in both light infantry and U.S. Army Ranger units. Following these initial assignments, he served as a staff officer and later as a company commander in the in 1-508th Airborne Battalion Combat Team in Vicenza, Italy. In 2001, COL Ellis returned to 2/75th Ranger Regiment. From 2001 to 2004, he served as the battalion logistics officer and Bravo Company commander completing several deployments in support of Operation ENDURING FREEDOM. Upon graduation from the U.S. Army Command and General Staff College in 2005, COL Ellis reported to 2/75th Ranger Regiment and served as the battalion executive officer and battalion operations officer. During this time, he conducted further deployments in support of both Operation ENDURING FREEDOM and Operation IRAQI FREEDOM. Following this assignment, COL Ellis reported to the Joint Special Operations Command at Fort Bragg, North Carolina, where he served from 2007 to 2010 as a current operations officer and executive officer to the Commander. COL Ellis assumed command of 1-501 Infantry (ABN) in Anchorage, Alaska, on June 28, 2010. While serving as the battalion commander, COL Ellis deployed the battalion for 10 months to Khost, Afghanistan, in support of Operation ENDURING FREEDOM. In June 2013, COL Ellis assumed command of 3/75th Ranger Regiment, a position he held until April 2015. During his time as the 3/75th commander, COL Ellis deployed twice to Operation ENDURING FREEDOM in Afghanistan. He is scheduled to take command of 2nd Cavalry Regiment (Stryker) in Vilseck, Germany, in July 2016. COL Ellis holds a bachelor's degree in Russian language from the U.S. Military Academy and a master's in management from Webster University.

LIEUTENANT COLONEL (LTC) ANTONIO M. PAZ was commissioned through the Reserve Officer Training Corps program at San Jose State University in 1994 as an infantry officer. He was assigned to the 1st Infantry Division in Schweinfurt, Germany, where he participated in deployments to Croatia and the NATO-led Implementation Force mission in Bosnia. He went on to join the 10th Mountain Division for another deployment to Bosnia and then commanded an infantry company and a brigade headquarters company. LTC Paz went on to receive training in psychological operations (PSYOP) and then information operations (IO). This training led to his tours as a tactical detachment commander deployed to Iraq; IO planner at the Joint Special Operations Command; two tours in Afghanistan; Battalion S3 at the 6th PSYOP Battalion (Airborne); division chief for Military Information and Support Operations (MISO) at Special Operations Command Europe. Most recently, LTC Paz commanded the 5th Battalion, 1st Special Warfare Training Group (Airborne) at Fort Bragg, NC. LTC Paz holds a bachelor's degree in history and is currently a member of the U.S. Army War College resident class of 2016. Upon promotion to colonel and his graduation, he will go on to serve in the Washington, DC, area prior to taking command of a MISO unit next year.

LIEUTENANT COLONEL (LTC) KYLE A. REED was commissioned as a second lieutenant in the infantry, and began his professional military career in 1996 as a Bradley fighting vehicle platoon leader and later as a battalion support platoon leader at Fort Stewart, Georgia. Following completion of the Infantry Officer Advance Course in 1999, he was assigned to the 1st Brigade Combat Team, 82nd Airborne Division at Fort

Bragg, North Carolina. While there, he served in a variety of assignments including as a brigade and battalion assistant operations officer, command of Alpha and Headquarters Companies, 2nd Battalion, 504th Parachute Infantry Regiment, and commander of the United States Army Advanced Airborne School. During these commands, he deployed once to Afghanistan and twice to Iraq in support of the Global War on Terror, 2003 - 2004. After completion of the Army's Command and General Staff College in 2007, he was assigned back to the 1st Brigade Combat Team, 82nd Airborne Division to serve as the operations officer and executive officer, 2nd Battalion, 504th Parachute Infantry Regiment. From 2007 to 2010, he deployed to Iraq for two year-long deployments. From 2010 to 2012, he served as an Infantry Branch assignment officer for majors and lieutenant colonels at Fort Knox, Kentucky. LTC Reed next served as a special assistant and speech-writer to the Commander, U.S. European Command/Supreme Allied Commander Europe. His last assignment was as the commander, 1st Squadron (Airborne), 91st Cavalry Regiment, 173rd Infantry Brigade Combat Team (Airborne) at Grafenwoehr, Germany. As a commander, he led operations in Atlantic Resolve, U.S. reassurance to the NATO Alliance and the Baltic Nations, and Fearless Guardian, a U.S. training mission in support of Ukraine military forces to increase the defense capabilities of their Nation. LTC Reed received his bachelor's degree in business administration from Appalachian State University in Boone, North Carolina in August 1995. In 2007, he completed his master's degree in business and organizational security management from Webster University.

LIEUTENANT COLONEL (Lt Col) LENDY "ALA-MO" RENEGAR first entered military service in 1991 as a U.S. Army National Guard intelligence analyst and was later commissioned through the U.S. Air Force ROTC program at North Carolina State University in 1994 with a bachelor's degree in meteorology. He holds a master's degree in aeronautics from Embry-Riddle Aeronautical University, Florida, and is a graduate of Air War College, Department of Distance Education. While commanding the 493d Fighter Squadron at Royal Air Force Lakenheath, his squadron won the 2014 Raytheon Trophy for the top Fighter Squadron in the U.S. Air Force (USAF) for its efforts in NATO's Baltic Air Policing and Icelandic Air Policing missions during the Russian invasion of Crimea. Lt Col Renegar commanded three deployed Air Expeditionary Groups for NATO and served as the chief of the commander's action group for the U.S. Air Forces in Europe. He has served in combat over the skies of Iraq and has piloted the F-15 aircraft in multiple operational active air scrambles and intercepts including the first night vision goggle identification of a Russian fighter in USAF history. Lt Col Renegar is currently a member of the U.S. Army War College resident class of 2016, upon completion of which he will serve as the chief of staff for the 438th Air Expeditionary Wing, Train-Advise-Assist-Command-Air (TAAC-AIR) in Kabul, Afghanistan.

LIEUTENANT COLONEL (Lt.Col.) JOHN T. VAUGHAN is an assault amphibious vehicle officer in the U.S. Marine Corps. He holds a master's degree in security studies (Europe and Eurasia) from the Naval Postgraduate School. He is a designated Eurasian regional area officer and a former accredited Marine

Attaché to Kyiv, Ukraine. Upon graduation from the U.S. Army War College, he will assume duties as deputy G-3, 5th Marine Expeditionary Brigade, in Manama, Bahrain.

SUMMARY

Over the past century, U.S. relations with Russia have evolved from ally to enemy to strategic partner to competitor. The political landscape and national interests of the Russian Federation have changed since the breakup of the Soviet Union. As a result, relations between Russia and the United States today are strained, largely because of Russia's actions in Ukraine. Understanding Russia's intentions has been challenging and difficult in the past for the United States. This monograph argues that Russia's foreign policy is driven by four overarching factors: Russian President Vladimir Putin's approach to the world around him; the Kremlin's desire for centralized control of the population; Russia's desire to protect its homeland through an outside "buffer zone;" and an enduring distrust of the West.

Given these drivers of Russian foreign policy, deterring Russia without provoking conflict or creating a spiraling security dilemma is a difficult task. Russia's actions in Crimea and eastern Ukraine have put the Baltic States and Eastern Europe on edge. The primary challenge for the United States and the North Atlantic Treaty Organization (NATO) is to deter both a conventional threat and an ambiguous[1] threat as Russia works toward achieving its objectives. The most dangerous scenario facing the West is a Russian advance into Alliance territory with conventional forces, but many assume this is not very likely. Alternatively, an indirect Russian approach using ambiguous warfare to fracture the Alliance and increase Russia's influence in Europe is far more likely.

In attempting to devise solutions that would address both a conventional and an ambiguous threat, this monograph theorizes that based on current force structure, NATO lacks the capability to defeat a surprise Russian conventional attack into the Baltic States or Eastern Europe, regardless of the likelihood of such a scenario. However, this does not preclude the need to enhance conventional capabilities, modify force posture, and develop additional capabilities to counter both conventional and ambiguous threats, which will in turn underpin credible deterrence against Russian aggression.

To develop such capabilities requires a concerted effort on the part of NATO, the European Union (EU), and their member states, with the United States playing a key role. Yet Washington cannot afford, through its efforts, to reassure allies to the point where they solely rely on the United States to ensure their security. Therefore, European NATO members should continue searching for more effective ways to increase capabilities and progressively increase their defense budgets. Meanwhile, the United States and its allies must employ a coordinated, whole of government effort to address capabilities beyond the scope of the military, such as law enforcement, that are critical to addressing an ambiguous threat. Additionally, the United States European Command (EUCOM) and the United States Army Europe (USAREUR) must more effectively align their security cooperation activities to support capability development, especially through NATO's defense planning process.

In doing these things, the United States and NATO must be careful that reassurance and deterrence activities, and associated policies, do not provoke further Russian aggression, or lead to a new security dilemma. To that end, any policy or strategy toward Russia must understand Russian intentions and the likelihood of a conventional attack — balanced against the reality of potential ambiguous activities and Russian influence in Europe.

In light of the key considerations outlined above, this monograph offers the following recommendations:

- The Department of Defense (DoD) should assign, allocate, and apportion forces versus aligning them, in support of EUCOM's Theater Campaign Plan and contingency plans.
- The U.S. Army should assign a Joint Task Force (JTF)-capable two-star headquarters (HQ) to USAREUR.
- The U.S. Army should establish a rotational allocation of an Armored Brigade Combat Team (ABCT) that provides a continuous armor presence in Europe.
- The U.S. Army should ensure its units receive the requisite security cooperation, and/or foreign internal defense-specific training for conventional units.
- The National Guard's State Partnership Program should focus more explicitly on building and maintaining allies' resiliency in the face of ambiguous warfare.
- EUCOM should re-examine its theater security cooperation (TSC) process to more effectively nest efforts between EUCOM and USAREUR.
    - EUCOM and USAREUR should more effectively make use of NATO capability targets, part of the NATO Defense Planning Process, to define the types of activities that will focus on lacking capabilities.
    - EUCOM should reduce the number of exercises in order to focus on high-quality, fully integrated NATO operations.

- EUCOM should synchronize country-specific sections of its Theater Campaign Plan (TCP) with the U.S. Embassy Integrated Country Strategies.
- EUCOM and USAREUR should ensure staffs are trained, particularly those involved in security cooperation, to conduct strategic and operational planning, and to understand the nesting of national security objectives with Alliance capability targets.
- The Joint Staff and the U.S. Army should improve manning levels of appropriate staff expertise to plan and manage the inform and influence activities at EUCOM, subordinate units, and within the proposed two-star HQ.
- The DoD and Department of State (DoS) should ensure they have effective mechanisms to coordinate information campaigns, and make necessary adjustments as the information environment evolves.
- The DoD should reconsider its representation at the U.S. Mission to the EU in order to enhance its ability to synchronize efforts with NATO and EUCOM.
- Washington needs to build a concerted effort among interagency partners to identify areas where the United States can assist European NATO members develop capabilities to deter Russia's ambiguous warfare.
- NATO should re-examine its Supreme Allied Commander Europe's (SACEUR) authority to reposition forces in Europe.
- NATO should move toward a NATO multinational logistics capability.

- NATO should streamline the timeline for approvals of counter-Russia actions.
- NATO should reinitiate dialogue with Russia.

ENDNOTES - SUMMARY

1. The use of the term "ambiguous" rather than the more common term of "hybrid" is discussed in Chapter 1, and is the term used throughout this monograph.

METHODOLOGY

The research for this project began with an in-depth study of available literature, to include a relatively vast amount of recent publications on Russia's resurgence and U.S. responses. It also included a series of research discussions with various staff civilian and military personnel at the Army Staff, the Office of the Secretary of Defense Staff, the U.S. Department of State, the U.S. Military Delegation to the North Atlantic Treaty Organization (NATO), the U.S. Mission to NATO, the NATO International Staff, the U.S. National Military Representative to Supreme Headquarters Allied Powers Europe (SHAPE) staff, the SHAPE staff, the United States Army Europe (USAREUR) staff, and the United States European Command (EUCOM) staff. The research also included discussions and vetting of initial findings with members of various Washington, DC-based think tanks.

INTRODUCTION

The post-Cold War peace dividend in Europe seems to be coming to an end. Russia is demonstrating its military might, and a very savvy ability to influence European politics, economics, and the media. Meanwhile, much of Europe remains dependent on Moscow for energy security, creating vulnerabilities that affect civilians as well as military activities and operations. Elsewhere, the refugee crisis and recent terrorist attacks in Paris and Brussels have put Europe on edge. In the face of a major threat from returning foreign fighters, several Schengen agreement countries have recently reinstituted border controls.

> *"In the afternoon of August 8, 2008, then-Russian President Dmitry Medvedev ordered the military to start the 'Operation to force Georgia to peace.' Russian aircraft destroyed Georgian military bases and airfields, and Russian tanks rolled into the republic, quickly ousting the Georgian forces and forcing them far into Georgian territory, stopping just short of the capital, Tbilisi. Infantry and paratroopers followed, securing control on the ground. By August 12, the military stage of the operation was over.*
>
> *The military casualties from the Russian side were over 70 people dead, while the Georgian military said they lost over 150 servicemen. Hundreds of people were wounded."*[1]

U.S. policymakers clearly face a multitude of national security challenges in Europe, and all deserve some level of attention from the National Security Council. However, and even though the security landscape is indeed evolving, the United States has made it clear that Europe is no longer its primary security concern. Instead, Washington continues to pursue the rebalance to Asia while keeping a watchful eye on the Middle East. The challenge lies in how to prioritize increasingly limited resources to address these global threats. Bringing this down to the regional level in Europe, the United States must prioritize how and with what it should respond to the increasing multitude of challenges in Europe. Washington will need to accept some level of risk, while asking its European allies and partners to do more. The European Union (EU) and the North Atlantic Treaty Organization (NATO) are both working to address the challenges associated with the refugee crisis and terrorism. NATO is also considering how best to deter an increasingly aggressive Russia, which

> *"In recent years, Russia has notably increased the size and frequency of its annual military exercises, and taken additional steps such as staging snap exercises and conducting surprise inspections of military units, steps aimed to improve the combat readiness of Russian forces for large-scale regional conflicts. Between February 2014 and September 2015, Russia conducted at least six snap exercises of various scope and size and two large-scale planned exercises involving forces in the Western, Central, and Southern Military Districts. A snap exercise in Kaliningrad consisted of 9,000 military personnel, along with hundreds of armored vehicles and artillery. Another snap exercise in the Western and Central Military Districts mobilized 150,000 personnel and the Baltic Fleet. These exercises demonstrate Moscow's ability to rapidly move military forces along its borders and pose an immediate concern to NATO's Eastern allies. Poland, for instance, was motivated to invoke Article 4 consultations at NATO headquarters in March 2014 given the perceived threat these exercises represented to its security."[2]*

will likely be a major theme at its upcoming summit in Warsaw in July 2016. While the United States remains concerned with the numerous challenges in Europe to its national security interests, and to its relationships with its allies and partners, actions clearly point to a focus on reassuring NATO allies and deterring Russian aggression in the Baltic States and Eastern

Europe. The United States recently sent a clear message with the dramatic funding increase for the European Reassurance Initiative in the President's proposed fiscal year 2017 budget, from just under $1 billion to $3.4 billion.

Acknowledging the many challenges in Europe and their potential impact on U.S. national security and that of European allies and partners, and recognizing the role of the Department of Defense (DoD) in securing national security objectives, this monograph focuses on the threat from a resurgent Russia to the Baltic States and Eastern Europe.

Russia Strengthens Western Military District.

"Russia's defense leadership has signaled that among its priorities for 2016 will be the creation of 'three divisions' in the Western Military District (MD): a move sure to ignite further speculation concerning Moscow's intentions toward its neighbors. This initiative has already prompted suggestions that it is a response to North Atlantic Treaty Organization (NATO) exercises in the Alliance's east. . . . On January 12, . . . Defense Minister Sergei Shoigu outlined some of the achievements of 2015 as well as the challenges ahead. In particular, he noted that during the previous year, the level of modern equipment and weaponry in the Armed Forces had increased to 47 percent, with the 2016 target set at 51 percent. Among the priority areas for the next 12 months, Shoigu gave prime position to . . . nuclear triad, continuing 'snap inspections' of the Armed Forces, improving strategic mobility, working on air defense. . .The idea that Shoigu had used the creation of three divisions in Western MD as a counter-move against NATO soon took hold in some Russian media coverage. Notably, an article by Aleksandr Goltz, the deputy editor of Yezhednevny Zhurnal, elevated Shoigu's priority for the 20th Army as the 'most important' issue facing the Armed Forces in 2016. . .

Clear evidence indicates that the General Staff uses the snap inspections to justify further changes to the Armed Forces, and in many cases quietly 'refine' the 'New Look' reforms. . .The latest reform in the Western MD is a limited or low-key effort to 'respond' to increased NATO activity, but its roots lie in the ongoing shifts in Russian military organization and trying to make sense of the reformed structures from the period 2008–2012."[3]

"On February 8, President Vladimir Putin ordered a 'snap inspection' military exercise in the Southern Military District (MD). . . . The pattern of snap inspection exercises in Russia is now well established, introduced in February 2013 by Defense Minister Army-General Sergei Shoigu in an effort to raise combat readiness in the Armed Forces. These exercises are used to assess units and test various aspects of the military. Massive snap exercises are also frequently used to send signals to other actors, as exemplified by their regular use following Russia's illegal annexation of Crimea in February–March 2014. . . . According to defense ministry sources, the main theme of the February snap inspection in the Southern MD was to rehearse the defense of the Crimean Peninsula from a "massive air attack." Consequently, the air force and air defense played a significant part. . . . However, the snap inspection in the Southern MD was staged in the context of an enduring period of tensions in Russia's relations with the United States as well as NATO, stemming from Moscow's behavior in Ukraine and disagreement over its intervention in Syria. Indeed, given heightened tensions between Ankara and Moscow since the Turkish downing of the Russian Su-24M bomber on November 24, 2015, the snap inspection may have been calibrated to showcase Russia's capability to respond to escalation, should the Turkish government take such risks. Moreover, the exercise coincided with Prime Minister Dmitry Medvedev warning about conflict escalation risks in Syria during the Munich Security Conference. Medvedev especially targeted his warnings toward other actors contemplating sending ground forces to the conflict in Syria. . .

Given the timing of the snap inspection, its composition, and the prominent role assigned to rebuffing an imaginary and highly improbable 'massive air attack' on Crimea, it is certainly possible that Russia's political-military leadership wants the exercise to convey a warning of escalation risks to foreign powers considering a more direct military role in Syria — and one that crosses Moscow's strategic aims and interest in the country. If so, that warning includes Turkey, a country covered by NATO's Article 5. . ." [4]

This monograph also addresses a specific element of Russian policy and strategy whilst recognizing that any U.S. policy or strategy toward Russia must consider the totality of Russia's actions. Such consideration is essential since Russian actions, while geographically focused, may actually be in response to perceived adversarial action in another geographic location (e.g. Russia action in the Arctic or the Middle East could be

> *"Approximately 600 paratroopers, from the 173rd Airborne Brigade, deployed for training rotations in Estonia, Latvia, Lithuania and Poland, April 23-28 [2014], to enhance ongoing military-to-military relationships and demonstrate assurance of America's commitment to its NATO allies. . . . April 24, paratroopers from Company A, 1st Battalion, 503rd Infantry Regiment, arrived in Riga, Latvia, to conduct small unit and leader training with members of the Latvian Land Forces Infantry Brigade. . . . At [a] ceremony, attended by Latvian Prime Minister Laimdota Straujumaas, as well as other senior officials and the American ambassador, Straujumaas said that by hosting paratroopers from the 173rd, 'one of the best American military's best,' Latvia feels NATO's solidarity and how important Latvia is to the other partners of the alliance. . . . On April 26, paratroopers from Company B, 1st Battalion, 503rd Infantry Regiment, 173rd Infantry Brigade Combat Team (Airborne), arrived at Siauliai Air Base in Lithuania, to begin training with the Lithuanian army's 'Iron Wolf' Mechanized Infantry Brigade at the Rukla training area. . . . 'These exercises send a strong message: We stay true to our word with our NATO allies,' said 2nd Lt. Joseph Dunfy, a paratrooper also with Company B. . .*
>
> *'This is an opportunity to reassure Lithuania that we are here to be committed to them and that we'll stand next to [our partners] no matter what,' said Sgt. Jonathan Grant, a paratrooper with Company B. . . . These training rotations 'are an obvious manifestation of the commitment between our countries and this alliance,' said [Maj. Gen. Richard C. Longo, deputy commanding general, U.S. Army Europe]."[5]*

in response to Allied action in Eastern Europe). Thus, policies and strategies must consider intended effects, potential Russian responses and reactions, as well as second and third order effects on Russia and other relevant actors. Policy and strategy should also address ways to preclude or mitigate unacceptable Russian behavior. Additionally, although Russia indeed possesses the capabilities to pose an existential threat to the United States, this monograph begins from the assumption that current Russian actions are not a direct existential threat to the United States, but rather are an existential threat to European security institutions, and in particular to NATO and the EU. If those institutions fail, then so could the current order in Europe with a potential second order effect that could significantly increase the threat to U.S. national security.

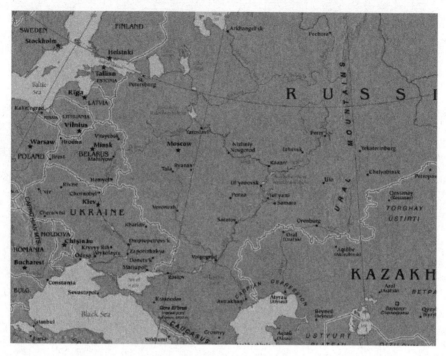

Source: Central Intelligence Agency

Figure I-1. Map of Russia.

This monograph includes recommendations on how and where the U.S. Army, U.S. European Command (EUCOM), and NATO should focus efforts to achieve defined effects. It does so fully recognizing that the United States has tried for many years to encourage its European NATO allies to pull a greater share of the burden. This monograph also recognizes that with global commitments, the United States can no longer afford to lift the bar from the allies when it becomes too heavy. While the solutions this monograph proposes may not be politically palatable for many allies, they must nevertheless be considered in light of the current trajectory in European security. Winning in a complex world requires the U.S. Army to help allies succeed in pulling their share of the burden. Looking beyond the Army, this monograph also addresses where the U.S. DoD and other interagency partners play a role. This monograph sets aside any discussion on the role of nuclear deterrence, focusing instead on the role of conventional forces. Finally, holistic solutions to respond to Russian resurgence go well beyond the scope of the military, where even partial military solutions require Joint action. Consequently, this monograph analyzes the situation primarily from a land-

Estonians were fully engaged in their independence celebration hosting a parade and air display in the capital city of Tallinn. The viewing platform was full of distinguished visitors, including a representative of the Russian Federation. The crowd was waiting on a North Atlantic Treaty Organization (NATO) fly-by that included four F-15 Eagle fighter jets from the U.S. Air Forces Europe. The Russian turned to the Estonian Air Chief with a smile and remarked that he expected the F-15s to be late. They weren't. A few minutes earlier, over 100 miles away, they had completed an intercept of a Russian Federation Air Force aircraft violating Estonian airspace. They escorted it out of Estonia's sovereign airspace and went supersonic over the Baltic Sea to make the fly-by on time much to the delight of the crowd. The Estonian ambassador to NATO, Lauri Lepik, later commented that the "intensity of Russian flights, and the fact that that they've been conducting patrols with strategic bombers, was completely unpredictable." Ambassador Lepik went on to say "I do not recall ever having a Russian strategic bomber flying around us." Russia is also using the land and maritime domains; in one instance in the spring of 2014, it deployed nearly 50,000 soldiers on the NATO's border in an unannounced snap exercise that appeared to "mimic a potential conflict with Europe." Lithuania and Estonia have expressed concern at the growing number (and type) of Russian Navy exercises in the Baltic Sea. [6]

power perspective, to include most of the considerations and recommendations proposed within it.

—Photo courtesy of Lt. Col. Rex "Lurch" Lewis

A U.S. Air Forces Europe (USAFE) assigned F-15C from the 493d Fighter Squadron out of Royal Air Force Lakenheath, UK intercepts a Russian Federation Air Force Aircraft during NATO's Baltic Air Policing Mission in 2014 shortly after the Russian invasion of Crimea. Forward-based combat power enabled these fighters to respond to trouble in the Baltics in under 14 hours, a time that European leaders insist can't be accomplished from the United States.

Figure I-2. F-15 Intercepts.

This monograph includes five primary chapters, followed by a concluding chapter. The first chapter frames the strategic environment in which Russia operates in order to provide a baseline understanding of its actions. It argues that effectively tempering Russia's actions in the future is best accomplished though the persistent use of the diplomatic and economic instruments of national power. Given the zero-sum mindset of Russian leaders, using the military instrument of power in an overt way is likely to lead to escalation and conflict. Nonetheless, the military instrument should be used in a nuanced, indirect fashion that strengthens and reassures NATO allies and partners and galvanizes the Alliance, emphasizing the fact that NATO is a deterrent to Russia. Taking into consideration Russia's willingness to use military force to achieve its objectives, the second chapter explores deterrence efforts. It does so in order to clearly define what deterrence is, and relies on the key tenants of deterrence theory to assess the United States' ability to deter Russian aggression in the Baltic States and Eastern Europe. It then identifies conventional deterrence solutions, which also sets the foundation for the subsequent three chapters.

Chapter 3 focuses on the time-distance challenge that a potential adversary could exploit to Washington's disadvantage, especially in the absence of robust indicators and warnings. It argues that two key force structure elements should be returned to U.S. Army Europe: an assigned two-star headquarters (HQ) and a rotationally allocated Armored Brigade Combat Team (ADCT) providing a continuous heel-to-toe presence of armor in Europe. These forces should remain in place until the strategic calculus changes again, for example, when Russia no longer threatens its neighbors or NATO's new Wales Summit initiatives are in place and ready to respond to further Russian aggression. The third chapter also argues that NATO should consider several steps to mitigate some of the time-distance challenges, including augmenting the authority of the Supreme Allied Commander in Europe (SACEUR), developing multinational logistics capabilities, and streamlining deployment approval processes.

Chapter 4 addresses how the Army and EUCOM can better leverage theater security cooperation (TSC), including foreign internal defense (FID), to build a credible conventional deterrent in Europe. It argues that the best way for NATO, EUCOM, and the U.S. Army to counter the most dangerous course of action posed by Russia without the return of large numbers of troops to Europe is through focused TSC, and in particular a refocusing of exercises in Europe.

Chapter 5 briefly examines U.S. and NATO operations in the highly contested information battle-space. It also highlights key areas of Russian propaganda, identifies shortfalls in U.S. abilities and areas of risk, and offers recommendations to mitigate the associated shortcomings. This monograph then concludes by highlighting key points and recommendations for senior leaders to consider.

ENDNOTES - INTRODUCTION

1. "5 years after 5-Day War: Russia and Georgia bury the hatchet," RT (website), August 7, 2013, available from *https://www.rt.com/politics/ossetia-georgia-russia-media-166/*, accessed April 4, 2016.

2. Kathleen H. Hicks *et al.*, *Evaluating Future U.S. Army Force Posture in Europe: Phase I Report*, Roman and Littlefield: New York, February 2016, pp. 2-3, available from *csis.org/files/publication/160203_Hicks_ArmyForcePosture_Web.pdf*, accessed February 24, 2016.

3. Roger McDermott, "Russia Strengthens Western Military District," *Eurasia Daily Monitor*, Vol. 13, Iss. 12, January 19, 2016, available from *www.jamestown.org/programs/edm/single/?tx_ttnews%5Btt_news%5D=44997&cHash=daa62f47a1dbb05ce883ba3ef c391fab#.Vv7IiqQrLic*, accessed April 1, 2016.

4. Roger McDermott, "Putin Orders 'Snap Inspection' Exercise in Southern Military District," *Eurasia Daily Monitor*, Vol. 13, Iss. 31, February 16, 2016, available from *www.jamestown.org/single/?tx_ttnews%5Btt_news%5D=45097&no_cache=1#.Vv7G-paQrLic*, accessed April 1, 2016.

5. A.M. LaVey, "173rd Paratroopers Arrive in Poland, Baltics for Unscheduled Exercises," The Official Homepage of the United States Army, April 30, 2014, available from *www.army.mil/article/125040/*, accessed April 1, 2016.

6. One of the authors commanded the NATO Baltic Air Police Mission from January 1, 2014 - May 1, 2014, during the Russian invasion of Crimea. High-ranking Lithuanian Air Force officers who were located on the viewing platform relayed this story to the same author.

7. *Ibid.*

8. Elisabeth Braw, "Bully in the Baltics: The Kremlin's Provocations," *World Affairs,* Vol. 177, No. 6, Mar-Apr 2015, p. 2.

9. *Ibid.*

10. "Russia Targets NATO with Military Exercises," *STRATFOR*, March 19, 2015, available from *https://www.stratfor.com/analysis/russia-targets-nato-military-exercises*, accessed March 21, 2016.

11. Damien Sharkov, "Conflict: Russian navy practices anti-submarine combat in Baltic and Arctic," *Newsweek*, July 10, 2015, available from *europe.newsweek.com/russian-navy-practices-anti-submarine-combat-baltic-arctic-330131*, accessed March 21, 2016.

CHAPTER 1

UNDERSTANDING RUSSIA'S AIMS THROUGH THE LENS OF VLADIMIR PUTIN, HISTORY AND CULTURE

Over the past century, U.S. relations with Russia have evolved from ally to enemy to strategic partner to competitor. Relations between Russia and the United States today are strained in light of Russia's actions in Ukraine as well as each actor's diverging interests. One question persists as the West tries to understand Russia. What motivates Russian President Vladimir Putin's foreign policy approach toward the United States and Eastern Europe and how can the United States influence Russia's foreign policy? The ability of the United States to understand Russia has been challenging and difficult in the past. Moreover, the political landscape and national interests of the Russian Federation have drastically changed since the breakup of the Soviet Union, North Atlantic Treaty Organization (NATO) enlargement, the Global War on Terror, and the current Islamic State in Iraq and Syria (ISIS) conflict in Syria.

The United States consistently misunderstands Russia's aims due to differences between U.S. and Russian political, social, and strategic culture. A common fallacy in U.S. foreign policy toward Russia is the belief that Russians think, behave, and make decisions like U.S. citizens. American policymakers are confused when Russian policymakers make decisions that are ambiguous and diverge from U.S. ideals and policy aims. Attempting to employ "mirror imaging" as a way of influencing Russian foreign policy is dangerous and has yielded little benefit.[1] The reset policy of 2009 validates the cognitive trap of mirror imaging specifically with the New Strategic Arms Reduction Treaty (START) of 2010. New START sought to mutually reduce nuclear arms and launchers between the United States and Russia. Applying the principle of mirror imaging, if Russia thought like the United States, then both parties would likely agree to diminish their nuclear arsenals equally as part of the compromise. Conversely, since Russia thinks differently than the United States and more so in the mindset of a zero-sum game, New START required cuts to the U.S. nuclear arsenal while not reducing that of Russia.[2]

Sun Tzu professes that one must know oneself and the enemy. If one knows neither then one is always in peril.[3] To understand the Russian mindset and influence it, one must be intimately familiar with the context of history, Russian/Soviet culture, and how these factors influence the Russian executive decision-making process. For example, the Russian desires to protect its homeland and a general distrust of outsiders have been unusually strong influences on Russian foreign policy. Careful examination of Russia's national interests as well as the previous decisions of Russian leadership to meet those ends can assist U.S. policymakers in developing successful strategies and policies to deal with the Russian Federation in the coming century.

In attempting to understand what has motivated and incentivized previous and current Russian leaders, this chapter argues that Russia's foreign policy toward the West is driven chiefly by four overarching concepts: the psychological background of President Putin and the evolution of his thought process; the desire for Russian domestic control of the population through a centralized government; a general, enduring distrust of the West; and protection of the Russian homeland through an outside "buffer zone."[4] After specifying the nature of these concepts, this chapter will then assess the diplomatic, informational, military, and economic tools most likely to influence Russia's foreign policy approach.

PUTIN: SHAPED BY CULTURE, HISTORY AND EXPERIENCE

The actions of President Putin illustrate decision-making trends of his foreign policy as well as his interactions with the United States and Europe. He has been called a tsar, an autocrat, and above all else a protector of the Russian Federation.[5] Putin's psychological background was shaped early in his career through Western interaction. Putin was the former head of Russian Federal Security Service, *Federalnaya Sluzhba Bezopasnosti* (FSB), a successor of the Committee for State Security *Komitet Gosudarstvennoy Bezopasnosti* KGB), and also a self-proclaimed *Chekist* (from the abbreviation for Extraordinary Commision, ChK) who spent a considerable amount of time outside of the Soviet Union in 1985-1990 in East Germany. *Chekists* view themselves as top leaders in Russia who orchestrate the political and economic well-being of the state.[6] Time spent out of Moscow proper gave Putin a more holistic approach to Russia's place in the international order.[7] He has a strong sense of national pride and order from his KGB background, but his posting outside of Russia has given him a unique perception of Europe and the West. From this peripheral position, Putin gained an acute awareness of the widening economic, technological, and strategic gaps between Russia and the West.[8] Putin saw this widening gap as a potential domestic threat. If the Russian population were exposed to a better way of life through economic

3

and technological advances, then surely an uprising inside Russia would ensue. This exposure may have shaped his views that the Russian population should be insulated from the West and strictly controlled to ensure Russia's preservation and status quo. Further, Putin's desire to control the Russian population stems from his sense of preserving the state and keeping the system intact.[9] This feeling of control and preserving the homeland was also evident in the way that Putin handled the conflicts in Dagestan and Chechnya in the late 1990s. Fearing the collapse of the Russian state, Putin moved Russian forces into Chechnya to keep Chechnya under Russian control. Should Chechnya gain independence, Putin feared it would only keep expanding and seize additional territories.[10]

Source: The White House, *https://www.whitehouse.gov/blog/2012/06/18/ bilateral-meeting-president-putin.*

Relations between the United States and Russia have become increasingly tense over the past decade. The actions of President Vladimir Putin illustrate decision-making trends of his foreign policy as well as his interactions with the United States and Europe.

Figure 1-1. U.S. President Barack Obama and Russian President Vladimir Putin.

Moving on from the FSB, Putin was appointed as Prime Minister in 1999. In 1999, President Boris Yeltsin stepped down and Putin became acting president. Putin came into the presidency in an era of instability and crisis. During Yeltsin's tenure as president, Russia was in a period of decline. Russia struggled to define itself in the aftermath of the breakup of the Soviet Union. Russian agricultural and industrial production was half of its previous output, and death rates increased as birth rates declined.[11] Russia's political leadership lacked stability, strength, and continuity. Economically, Russia was trending downward. This was evident in several areas such as the country's search for a post-Soviet identity and purpose, ineffective governance, and rampant corruption.[12]

Putin represented a much-needed return to stability and competence in governance and foreign policy, which was a stark contrast to Yeltsin's mismanagement of foreign policy and string of domestic policy failures. Yeltsin's presidency was plagued by failure to enact reforms in several key areas ranging from military and security reforms to energy sector and social entitlements.[13] To the Russian people, Putin represented a return to an idealized world of stability and order.[14] Putin moved away from Yeltsin's ad-hoc management style and used his influence to return a significant amount of power back to the executive branch. Putin's pragmatic leadership style has centered on one of centralized control and consistency.[15]

Because of Putin's strong hand and institution of centralized government or a *vertikal vlasti*, he continues to enjoy popular Russian support. *Vertikal vlasti* is the single line of power that emerges from the executive branch of the Russian president down to federal and provincial levels of government. Additionally, a *vertikal vlasti* reduces the system of checks and balances on the executive by the legislative and judicial branches of government. Use of the single line of power has enabled Putin to advance his agenda, reduce opposition to his policies and maintain control of the Russian population, as well as maintain control of the strategic narrative in his foreign policy actions, a point that Chapter 5 will further explore.

The enduring theme in Putin's first term as president was that of a savior.[16] The Russian population saw him as restoring order to governance, and establishing national identity and international rapport. The West saw him as a competent and amenable person. Putin's rhetoric at this time was European leaning—he espoused that Russia was a European nation and was receptive to discussions on European security and economic integration.[17] Putin's initial aims were twofold—a calculated approach to restore Russian stability to government and a strategic approach to restore Russia's former status in the international order. Putin has often been compared to Louis XIV and his mantra regarding France, *"L'état c'est moi"* ("I am the State"). Putin was seen domestically as a leader who was reviving Russia, but some questioned whether his policies would change under his successor.

Dmitry Medvedev was Putin's protégé and hand-picked successor in 2008, much as Putin was chosen by Yeltsin. Similar to the Yeltsin years, prime ministers have been appointed and presidential successors are chosen prior to any democratic election. Because of this, there typically has not been a significant change in Russian governance from president to president since the breakup of the Soviet Union. Moreover, it seems highly unlikely that Russian policy will change dramatically whenever Putin leaves the political stage, which is a key assumption in developing long-term policies and strategies toward Russia.

Additionally, studies of previous "democratic" processes in Russia illustrate a far different type of democracy than what is typically observed in the West. In Russia, democracy is more illiberal and managed. The system of government is more autocratic with elements of democracy. Democratic institutions such as free and fair elections and freedom of speech are "managed" in Russia to "maintain order."[18] The term hybrid regime is often used to describe the Russian Government with a combination of authoritarian and diminished democratic elements. The opposition to the incumbent rarely prevails, because it is difficult to mobilize enough support to wage a campaign in the extremely limited political space that the government makes available to "opposition" forces.

In the case of Dmitry Medvedev's presidency, there were very few deviations from Putin's previous security policies.[19] In his policy "National Security Strategy until 2020," Medvedev stated that Russia should emphasize multi-polarity in a U.S.-dominated unipolar system, openness to diplomacy (even with the West), protection of Russians wherever they may live, and the assumption that Russia has privileged interests in the near abroad.[20] Medvedev's presidency was receptive to diplomacy with the West, yet it was also tempered with caution and distrust.

In essence, Medvedev's foreign and security policy did not vastly differ from that of Putin.[21] Furthermore, Putin remained in the Russian Government as prime minister to monitor and mentor his successor. Medvedev's presidency and security policies were remarkably consistent with the Putin years. Overall, Medvedev was criticized for an inability to gain control of his security administration's apparatus during the tenure of his presidency. He did not wield the same power and control inside of the *vertikal vlasti* as Putin.[22] This became clear during the 2008 Georgia-South Ossetia crisis when no Russian executive decisions were made until Prime Minister Putin returned from the Olympic Games in Beijing.

Although not as effective as Putin, Medvedev did set the conditions in his security strategy for the international community to perceive Russia as a country that had persevered and overcome its domestic issues, was recovering economically and should be a peer amongst other world powers.[23] Above all else, both Putin and Medvedev shared another common goal, to remain in power and to see Russian aims realized. Both leaders saw the need to maintain and preserve a veneer of legitimate governance that the Russian people could rely upon at any cost.[24] The Western version of a legitimate government implies a system that elects its leaders through competitive elections, the presence of civil society, and an adherence to "rule of law." Both Medvedev and Putin encouraged legitimacy with the ultimate goal to stay in power, but their actions run counter to a truly Western legitimate democratic government. Elections in Russia have never been truly competitive, free, or fair, and Russian control of the media continues.

Each leader viewed the loss of control domestically as a loss of international respect. Both Putin and Medvedev believed that the appearance of a legitimate government must be maintained both at home and in the near abroad in order to quell the threat of a democratic uprising in Moscow. Neither Putin nor Medvedev wanted another color revolution happening in Moscow as they had in Kiev, Tbilisi, or Bishkek.

According to the 2009 Russian security strategy and analysis by Dr. Hans-Henning Schroder, a professor at the University of Bremen, "an 'orange scenario' — a development resembling that in Ukraine in 2004/2005 — is just as unacceptable to the Medvedev Administration as it was to Putin at the time."[25] Emerging color revolutions in Russia's near abroad have increased Putin's distrust of Western democracy, which he associates with a loss of order and control.

RUSSIAN DOMESTIC CONTROL IS STRATEGICALLY IMPORTANT

The Kremlin believes that a loss of internal control gives the perception of weakness and diminishes Russia's international stature.[26] Maintaining control of the population has been a cornerstone of Soviet and Russian governance. It has been a common thread from Yuri Andropov's tenure as General Secretary of the Communist Party of the Soviet Union in 1983 to President Putin's three presidential terms. Soviet and Russian leaders have consistently believed that opposition and dissidence leads to violent uprising, a loss of control and weakening of the state.[27] Putin maintains domestic control through the implementation of the *vertikal vlasti*, media control, and targeted violence to suppress dissidents. Recalling the Yeltsin years of the Russian presidency where disorder, economic collapse, and corruption abounded, Putin in his first term, implemented measures to reign in provincial leaders and other branches of government to restore order.[28]

Under the Putin Administration, control remains an integral part of his leadership style. Additionally, Putin has heavily influenced the State Duma[29], Russia's lower house of parliament, by eliminating the voting process for individual candidates. Voters can only vote via party lists for political parties, rather than individual candidates. The Duma has discretion to appoint party leaders arbitrarily.[30] More importantly, international institutions such as the Organization for Security and Cooperation (OSCE) consider elections in Russia unfair. The OSCE found fault on four counts with Russia's 2007 parliamentary elections and viewed these elections as neither free nor fair.[31]

Putin has also compromised independence of the judicial branch, subordinating it to the elites' perception of state interests. Putin's Russia can be summarized and graded on its level of freedom compared to other countries by its Freedom House rankings. Freedom House, a non-profit organization dedicated to spreading freedom and democracy ranks Russia as a "6" in political rights and civil liberties,[32] with "1" representing the most free and "7" the least free. Furthermore, Putin has taken great measures to retain control, reduce democratic processes, and suppress the opposition in Russia.

Moreover, under Putin, there have been several cases of targeted violence to control the opposition. Specific examples include the murders of Anna Politkovskaya, an outspoken journalist and political rights activist in 2006, and Boris Nemtsov, leader of the opposition in 2015. Both were outspoken in their opposition of President Putin and their murders speak volumes of the Russian population's willingness to accept silence and cooperate.[33] Anne Applebaum, Pulitzer Prize-winning author and noted journalist on communism, ascertains that because of Putin's strong beliefs for the good of the state and desire for control, dissidents must be "carefully controlled through legal pressure, public propaganda and if necessary targeted violence.[34]" Putin has a long-standing distrust of the dissidents and has suppressed them effectively though media control and the fear effect through targeted violence.[35] Furthermore, Putin is threatened by the rhetoric of Western democracy and views it as a catalyst to incite revolution from domestic Russians.[36]

A RUSSIAN LEGACY OF WESTERN MISTRUST

Russia's distrust of Western democracy is not a new concept. This distrust is heavily steeped in Soviet leadership culture and also in Putin's upbringing. One of Putin's mentors was Yuri Andropov, General Secretary of the Communist Party of the Union of Soviet Socialist Republics (USSR) from 1982-1983. Andropov also served as director of the KGB from 1967-1982. During Putin's first presidency, he erected several plaques to honor Andropov. Andropov largely believed in population control, strict order, and suppression of the Soviet dissident movement.[37] Andropov was also considered to be a protector of the ideals and interests of the communist state, much like Putin. Further, both men witnessed similar events that would forge their personal disdain toward democracy and dissident uprisings. Andropov witnessed this during the Hungarian uprisings in 1956. Putin had the same experience in Dresden with the ransacking of the Stasi police in 1989. Consequently, both men formed opinions that democracy leads to protest and protest leads to the destruction of law and order.[38] They believe that the Russian homeland must be protected at all costs from the threats that emerge from dissidence and Western ideals. Moreover, Putin blames the West for a myriad of issues ranging from a reduction in arms control agreements to fomenting attacks on Russian soil and the creation of al-Qaeda and the Taliban. He made telling comments during his "new world order" speech at Sochi denouncing the United States in 2014.

> From here emanates the next real threat of destroying the current system of arms control agreements. And this dangerous process was launched by the United States of America when it unilaterally withdrew from the Anti-Ballistic Missile Treaty in 2002…They (United States) once sponsored Islamic extremist movements to fight the Soviet Union. Those groups got their battle experience in Afghanistan and later gave birth to the Taliban and al-Qaeda.[39]

CREATING A BUFFER ZONE TO PROTECT THE HOMELAND

Defense of the homeland is a central theme in several countries' national security strategies, but this concept intensely drives Russian foreign policy, and is critical to developing logical and effective military strategies to deal with Russia. Russia's version of homeland defense extends much farther than Russia's natural borders and permeates into the former Soviet republics. To defend the homeland, Russia desires a buffer zone to expand its borders and protect displaced Russians.[40] Under Putin's leadership, Moscow protects these communities of ethnic Russians, known as the Russian diaspora.[41] The diaspora concept prevails in Putin's foreign policy toward Crimea, Georgia, and Ukraine and further enables Russia's effective use of hybrid warfare (sometimes referred to as gray zone challenges[42]) in an ambiguous manner, which this monograph will refer to as ambiguous warfare.[43] Protection of the Russian diaspora may influence the Russian decision-making process. Russian President Medvedev's security and foreign policy of 2009 made several mentions of protecting ethnic Russians abroad and asserted that Russia has privileged interests in certain regions, such as the former Soviet space.[44] Furthermore, Russia asserts entitlement in protecting ethnic Russians in its near abroad (Central and Eastern Europe, the Caucasus, Central Asia and the Baltic States) and views Western intervention as an affront to Russia.

Why is a Buffer Zone So Critical?

The Kremlin and Russian leadership feel compelled to maintain a "buffer zone" around its borders as a security measure to prevent the violation of Russian sovereign territory. Russian security thinking ascertains that the country is surrounded by enemies and must create a buffer zone against these outside threats.[45] This is a logical response for a country that has experienced invasion and occupation throughout its entire history from the Mongol invasion of Kievan Rus in 1223, to the Polish invasion of 1609, to Napoleon's destruction of Smolensk in the Great Patriotic War of 1812. Throughout history, Russia has been invaded, occupied, and forced to adopt different cultures. Over time, this has created the Russian perception of distrust of outsiders, isolation, and an overall intense xenophobia. This distrust and fear of encirclement manifests itself in Russia's tense relationship with NATO during periods of NATO enlargement,[46] especially with the entrance of countries formerly in Russia's near abroad.

Despite the West's best effort, Putin and the Kremlin have consistently viewed NATO as an "anti-Russian" security institution and an organization that habitually reduces Russia's buffer space through NATO enlargement actions. In the waning years of the 20th century and into the 21st century, Russia was invited to cooperate with international institutions. Although Russia indeed participated in various institutions as an invited partner, its influence was minimized due to the simple fact that it was not a voting member, particularly in NATO and the European Union (EU). NATO was specifically addressed in Russia's current National Security Strategy with language stating "plans to extend the Alliance's military infrastructure to Russia's borders, and attempts to endow NATO with global functions that go counter to norms of international law, are unacceptable to Russia.[47]"

Periods of NATO enlargement have consistently decreased the territory between Moscow and the West, which according to the Russian narrative, has threatened Russian security.[48] This expansion of new NATO members extended all the way to Russia's western border. NATO also sought to include Russia by inviting it to join the North Atlantic Cooperation Council in 1991; the Partnership for Peace program in 1994; establishing the NATO-Russia Founding Act in 1997; and establishing the NATO-Russia Council in 2002.[49] Yet what the West thought was an opportunity for promoting democratic values, increasing security, and building peaceful relationships became a point of contention for Russia.[50] NATO's expansion denied Russia its buffer zone, and placed NATO within 75 miles of St. Petersburg. Russia increasingly saw this as a loss of its buffer zone and a perceived expansion of U.S. and NATO influence in global security issues (e.g., Balkans, Iraq, Afghanistan, the NATO Mediterranean Dialogue, and the Istanbul Cooperation Initiative), while marginalizing its influence.[51] As Robert Kaplan, a senior fellow at the Center for a New American Security, notes, NATO actions further raised Russian concerns as it provoked historical memories of humiliating invasions by outsiders.[52] History matters to Russians and Russia's need for security is deeply rooted in its history. Add to that all that the shame of a lost empire with the collapse of the Soviet Union, it is easy to understand why Russia was not happy with the developing situation. During a decade of decline, Russia could only wait until it was in a position to do something about it.

Russian Use of Armed Forces and Other Means to Protect its Interests.

Russia, and in particular Putin, wants to regain its influence and limit what it perceives as security threats on its borders. Russia knows it is not the world power today it was during the Cold War, yet it is willing to give up a lot to regain this sense of security.[53] In an effort to reduce what it perceives as a security threat in its near abroad, Russia is looking for ways to create its own rules that would give it primacy. According to Stephen Covington, the long-time International Affairs Advisor to the Supreme Allied Commander Europe (SACEUR), Russia further believes that to compete with the other great powers, it needs to be able to influence fundamental change within the security, energy, economic, and financial systems that surround it.[54] Although its methods to operationalize its strategy are not new,[55] Russia is creating a new, dynamic, strategic security environment that creates unique challenges for U.S. national security policy and strategy.

Although Russia can employ many approaches in support of its goals, for discussion they are best simplified into three courses of actions: most likely, most disruptive, and most dangerous.

Based on recent history, the most likely Russian course of action, an ambiguous warfare attack against one of the allies or partners in the region, could consist of information operations, limited covert special operations, and instigated civil unrest. Russia has already employed this course of action three times in recent history, with its illegal annexation of Crimea, its operations in eastern Ukraine, and its efforts in Georgia. Russia's past success in employing ambiguous operations is likely to embolden their use in the future. The technique of inciting a Russian minority in a former Warsaw Pact or near abroad country and leveraging real (or more likely fabricated) 'oppression' as a pretext for Russian involvement has served Moscow well.[56] Russia could use these attacks to generate confusion, spur a request for Russian assistance, or to deliberately cause a state to fail—allowing for a Russian-friendly government to take over. Ambiguous challenges, such as these, may be difficult to attribute to the Russian state, and would likely capitalize on the struggle within NATO to build a consensus for an immediate response. NATO considers civil unrest and most other ambiguous operations as internal security issues, which should be dealt with as a national responsibility under Article 3 of the North Atlantic Treaty.[57] The key to countering this type of action is to build resilient allies in the border states that are able to absorb/counter this type of action internally or that are able to ascribe responsibility to Russia.

In addition to assessing the most likely or the most dangerous course of action, NATO must also consider the most disruptive. This course of action, while it may ultimately assist with achieving the sponsor nation's goals in the short term, serves to keep the targeted nation(s) off balance and focused internally.[58] In the context of Russia in Europe, the most disruptive course of action likely would be for Moscow to continually challenge the Alliance by conducting actions that would cause it to convene the North Atlantic Council (NAC) for potentially contentious deliberations.[59] All actions would remain below the Article 5 of the North Atlantic Treaty threshold and repeated deliberations would put strain on Alliance members and NATO, generating "Putin fatigue." These actions would target what both the Russians and NATO see as the center of gravity of the Alliance—the commitment of all members to Alliance-wide collective defense. While it is unlikely these actions would actually fracture the Alliance, they would certainly be disruptive and would put a strain on Alliance members.[60] The disruptive effect would come from members focusing on ambiguous actions, while potentially ignoring or minimizing real threats to NATO's territorial integrity. The best defense for NATO against this most disruptive course of action would be to recognize it and for all members to remain committed to collective defense of the Alliance.

The most dangerous course of action in Europe would be a conventional cross-border attack by Russia into NATO territory. Many authors have recently speculated on what exactly that would look like and under what pretenses it would occur. For the purposes of this monograph, the difference between the ambiguous warfare option and the conventional option is the presence of attributable Russian soldiers in the territory of another country, most likely the Baltic States. This is the most dangerous course of action for several reasons. First, "Russia's military can rapidly field substantial numbers of high-quality conventional forces in the Baltic states....and can do so far faster than NATO can surge equivalent or superior forces garrisoned in Central and Western Europe, let alone those in North America."[61] In numerous war games run by RAND analyst and former Department of Defense (DoD) official, David Ochmanek, in a Baltic attack scenario, Russia was able to invade, seize, and establish an Anti-Access Area Denial (A2/AD) bubble over the territory, making it incredibly challenging to get additional forces and logistics on the ground to assist with the fighting. Out of 16 iterations of the war game, the Alliance was unable to adequately defend the Baltic States.[62]

Russian's actions in the 2008 invasion of Georgia and its annexation of Crimea in 2014 surprised the international community and demonstrated its use of these courses of action in achieving its objectives. Looking at them more closely, it is clear that familiarity with the Russian executive mindset would validate Russia's invasion of Georgia and Ukraine, given Russia's rhetoric under President Medvedev and his security strategy.[63] As noted, Russian leaders place tremendous importance on defending the homeland and protecting the Russian diaspora abroad. In the 2008 Russo-Georgian conflict, Moscow claimed that it was merely protecting ethnic Russians living in South Ossetia and Abkhazia, who were being attacked by Georgian forces. Additionally, Putin later commented at the 2014 Valdai symposium in Sochi, Russia, that the Georgian conflict and more importantly the annexation of Crimea in 2014 were legitimate actions for Russia due to the right of self-determination.

The second point has to do with our actions in Crimea. I have spoken about this on numerous occasions, but if necessary, I can repeat it. This is Part 2 of Article 1 of the United Nations' Charter – the right of nations to self-determination. It has all been written down, and not simply as the right to self-determination, but as the goal of the United Nations.[64]

Examining Putin's comments from Valdai, he saw the situation in Ukraine collapsing rapidly in February 2014 and deemed it necessary to intervene. Specifically, Putin believed that Ukrainian President Viktor Yanukovych was losing control of the country. Putin was sensitive to the Russian diaspora in Crimea and its requests to the Kremlin to be protected from Ukrainian civil unrest. Putin believed his actions in Ukraine were justified because Nikita Krushchev illegally gave Crimea as a gift to Ukraine in 1954.[65] Putin ultimately believes that Crimea belongs to Russia and that the UN Charter allows him to protect the ethnic Russian diaspora that makes up the majority of Crimea's population. Putin's narrative is carefully crafted to put a veneer of legitimacy on Russia's actions. However, these actions violate international laws and norms.

Similarly, to achieve its objectives, Russia has demonstrated its willingness to use conventional military force, along with other ambiguous warfare. As described by Dave Johnson, a NATO International Staff member in the Defence (sic) Policy and Planning Division, Russia's approach includes a broad scope—encompassing diplomatic, informational, cyber, military and economic dimensions. It further seeks strategic depth by targeting adversaries' centers of gravity, while at the same time exercising strategic patience in such a way that it operates on unpredictable timelines.[66] Johnson refers to Russia as being in conflict with the West at a level short of openly declared war.[67] Covington notes that Russia's strategy uses the array of national power in an attempt to break apart and delegitimize European security institutions.[68] In doing so, Russia is keen not to provoke the United States or NATO to a point of open armed conflict; by employing an ambiguous approach. According to Doug Mastriano, a faculty member of the U.S. Army War College, an ambiguous approach includes not confronting NATO directly, leveraging deception to retain strategic agility, and gradually reasserting influence without resorting to war.[69] Frank Hoffman, a Washington-based national security analyst and senior research fellow at the National Defense University, similarly highlights Russia's use of national and subnational instruments of power to achieve objectives without crossing the conflict threshold in an attempt to extend its influence without triggering an armed response.[70] In so doing, Russia seeks to discredit NATO and ultimately fracture the Alliance, thus threatening European security.[71]

Russia's ambiguous strategy in Europe is comprehensive and includes capitalizing on European reliance on energy supplies, using the media as an influencing mechanism, influencing local and EU politicians, and leveraging ethnic Russian minorities. Russia conducts these activities below the provocation threshold, thus making it challenging to detect or to attribute any malicious intent to actions. The *2016 Global Forecast* by the Center for Strategic and International Studies (CSIS) cites examples of just how comprehensive Russia's ambiguous approach is. The forecast cites the recent creation of the Europe of Nations and Freedom (ENF) faction in the European Parliament that consistently votes in support of Russian positions, and whose leader received a a €9 million loan from the Moscow-based First Czech-Russian Bank in November 2014. Russia is increasing its television, radio, and Internet incursions in Europe, to include buying up many of Europe's independent news outlets. According to CSIS, these outlets target society via popular music and using human-interest stories to report on ways the West is in decline and portraying events in Ukraine that stoke fear among the populace. The media outlets also twist the relationship between the United States and Europe by suggesting that Europe is subservient to the United States.[72] Finally, European dependence on energy resources opens doors for Russian influence and leverage, particularly on the NATO periphery.[73] Kaplan draws similar conclusions.[74] With its ambiguous approach, and focus on enhancing its military capabilities,[75] Russia creates a unique and challenging problem for policy makers and strategists.

INSTRUMENTS OF NATIONAL POWER INFLUENCE RUSSIA DIFFERENTLY

Instruments of national power—diplomatic, information, military, and economic (DIME)—can influence Russia's behavior but some instruments are more effective than others. This is of particular note considering the Russian zero-sum mindset, in which Russia's loss is the opponent's gain and vice versa. In recent events however, the Russian zero-sum mindset is perhaps not absolute, evident with the Russian military pullout in Syria, which highlights the need to consider an approach that uses all instruments of national power. Diplomatic and economic instruments are strategic levers that have had some level of success on

Russia, while the direct conventional military instrument of power has proven to be the least effective and will most likely lead to conflict escalation. Some carefully calibrated elements of the military instrument do have merit and are effective in strengthening NATO and its partner countries. Some of these aspects will be explored in greater depth in the following chapters, as will an in-depth exploration of the use of the information element of national power, set aside exclusively for Chapter 5, to mitigate risks associated with the approaches addressed throughout this monograph.

Effective Use of the "D" in DIME.

Diplomacy between Russia and the United States has been somewhat restored following the reset policy of 2009.[76] Little credit has been given to the reset policy since it did not result in compromises on missile defense in Europe or NATO expansion. However, restoring diplomatic channels was important. The reset laid the foundation for dialogue between the United States and Russia that contributes to the framework for the two countries to co-exist, and perhaps eventually become strategic partners. Often, U.S. policy toward Russia has faltered because of the poor state of diplomacy between the the two countries.

Specifically, a lack of diplomacy contributed to Russian nuclear escalation during Operation ABLE ARCHER in 1983, where Russia misinterpreted a NATO exercise as an impending U.S.-led nuclear attack.[77] The 2009 reset aimed to repair U.S.-Russian relations, which were at an all-time low during the George W. Bush administration and Putin's first term as president.[78]

The United States should pursue a diplomatic approach with Russia that allows for strategic cooperation in areas of converging interests. Celeste Wallander, Special Assistant to the President and Senior Director for Russia and Eurasia on the National Security Council, stated, "we keep the door open with Russia to work in areas such as non-proliferation, nuclear and weapons of mass destruction (WMD) security, combating violent extremism and terrorism."[79] These are areas in which the United States can partner with Russia to enhance diplomacy and advance strategic partnering. Current U.S. policy toward Russia desires a Russia that is secure, prosperous and also a constructive stakeholder in the international system.[80] With Russia, the United States can and should agree to disagree on certain issues, but the fact remains that Russia's nuclear capability makes it a more desirable strategic partner than a strategic adversary. There is much to lose with continued misperceptions resulting from poor dialogue between the two countries. The United States must face the challenge of working with the Russia it faces and not the Russia it hopes for.[81]

The Critical Nature of the "M" in DIME.

The military instrument of U.S. national power can be used effectively to indirectly influence Russia if it is scaled appropriately. The military instrument of national power is effective against Russia when used in a smaller continuum, such as theater security cooperation (TSC). These efforts work in concert to reassure NATO partner nations, improve their capability, and have a deterring effect on Russia. The nexus of the U.S. European Command (EUCOM) Theater Strategy focuses on six priorities, the top two being deterrence of

Russian aggression and enabling the NATO Alliance.[82] Multilateral exercises with NATO partners, such as those conducted under the auspices of Operation AT-LANTIC RESOLVE and exercise Fearless Guardian, increase bilateral cooperation and interoperability and promote freedom of movement. Additionally, these exercises are designed to increase NATO allies' resilience to outside threats and strengthen core functions to support NATO Article 3 (self-defense) and Article 5 (collective defense) responsibilities. This lesser scale of the military instrument provides resiliency and strengthens NATO, which can deter Russia. Indeed, the very existence of a strong NATO is a deterrent to Russia, a point further explored later in this monograph.

The full-scale military response is the least preferred option due to the Russian mindset and the assumption that it will match military power with military power, leading to a security dilemma.[83] This was the impetus for the Cold War and illustrated how a zero-sum mindset incentivized Russia to escalate until the other side capitulates. During the Cold War, Russia continued to escalate with nuclear weapons procurement until it was no longer feasible to do so economically. Russia exhausted its economic capital completely to maintain pace with U.S. military spending.

Conventionally, Putin has continued to modernize Russia's military to create a more capable force. Today, Russia can deploy professional, capable military forces rapidly to the Baltic States or the Black Sea and can mobilize faster than NATO forces.[84] This is all the more reason why using the full spectrum of the military instrument of national power is not a suitable option.

Moreover, the military instrument may not deter Russia's use of ambiguous warfare.[85] Russia has readily used military forces in areas of its near abroad, chiefly against non-NATO members (Georgia and Ukraine) in instances of ambiguous warfare with little to no consequences in terms of Western military reactions. Russia's ambiguous warfare creates challenges for deterrence because they do not invoke a NATO Article 5 response, nor does the West view Russia's actions as grave enough to intervene directly with the military instrument of national power. Clearly Russia has vital interests in the near abroad, whereas U.S. interests are secondary at best. Russia's actions do have a destabilizing effect on NATO and have caused trepidation in several NATO members (chiefly the Baltic States of Lithuania, Latvia and Estonia, as well as Poland). Today, Russia uses ambiguous warfare to destabilize other actors where it believes the West would tolerate such aggression (e.g. Georgia and Ukraine).[86]

Full military engagement and conventional warfare against Russia would be an ineffective lever against Russia. This position will be explained in later chapters. Simply put, use of conventional warfare against Russia is ineffective because it could lead to an escalation of force and eventual full-scale warfare. The best strategy to fight Russia conventionally is not to begin the fight at all. Yet the Alliance must demonstrate to Russia, and other adversaries, that it is capable and willing to defend its members when needed.

Leveraging the "E" in DIME.

Using the economic instrument of national power has had some effect on Russia's behavior. Russian foreign policy — and specifically its ability to project power and gain international prestige — largely depends on Russia's economic growth and its ability to generate revenue to modernize.[87] The West has signaled unified disapproval of Russia's actions in Ukraine by supporting EU sanctions on Russia, which have hindered Russia's domestic economy.

This limited response has been typical of the current U.S. Administration's position toward Russia. The question remains of how effective the EU sanctions have been toward Russia in response to its actions in Ukraine. Putin found the sanctions more of a nuisance and has not really changed Russia's position toward Ukraine, but the sanctions have opened Putin and Russia to further diplomacy and cooperation. In his 2014 "World Order" speech in Sochi, Putin stated that the EU sanctions were a hindrance and designed to force Russia into backwardness, however the sanctions would not dissuade Russia from pursuing continued dialogue with Europe and the United States.[88] One unknown factor is how far Putin will allow the Russian economy to weaken before he changes his foreign policy. His rhetoric of Russian nationalism and Western culpability only strengthens the Russian domestic appetite to endure a declining economy.

To influence Russia, one must influence its economy, since economic power is the basis of its ability to maintain the Russian status quo and project power. Russia has continued to use its economy and status as an energy supplier to influence European countries. Furthermore, Putin has used economic pressure on Russian energy dependent countries in the EU to vote against renewing the EU sanctions through 2016.[89] Economic sanctions will take time before they can influence Russia's foreign policy. The key to success lies in their patient application and ability to hurt the Russian elite and middle class.[90] Russia continues to counter the EU sanctions and has imposed retaliatory measures on EU trading partners. However, recent data suggests that Russia's failing economy has had minimal impact on the EU.[91] Furthermore, falling oil prices, the declining ruble, and the EU sanctions will have long-term effects on Russia's economic capital and growth.[92] The potential adverse impact of sanctions on the Russian economy is estimated at 8-10 percent of gross domestic product (GDP) and that on the EU economy at some 0.5 percent of GDP.[93] Over time, all of these factors coupled together will have an adverse effect on Russia's economy and have the best potential to cause a shift in Russia's foreign policy.

CONCLUSION

Understanding Russian foreign policy aims and more importantly, what drives Putin's decision-making process is critical for influencing Russia's foreign policy. There has been considerable speculation that Russia's foreign policy could perhaps change with a different president. This is highly unlikely as the incumbent habitually continues the foreign policy aims of the previous administration. Furthermore, Russia's managed style of democracy does not allow the opposition to gain sufficient support or mobilize in either the executive or legislative branches. The executive branch continues to be the most powerful branch of government and controls the executive and judiciary as well as Russia's provincial leaders through the *vertikal vlasti* system.

The illusion of a strong Russia internationally is a critical component of its foreign policy. Domestic policy is largely tied to Russia's foreign policy and the perception that Russia is still a dominant, credible state actor. Russia believes that a loss of internal control gives the perception of weakness and consequently a loss of international respect. United States and European actions that discredit or vilify Russia will erode U.S.-Russian relations. United States diplomacy toward Russia should be a firm yet cooperative approach, as Putin is a pragmatist.

Russia's desire to protect its homeland and the Russian diaspora will continue to present foreign policy challenges to the United States. Russia continually uses the rhetoric of self-determination to protect these entities even when they fall outside Russia's borders. Russia's version of homeland defense extends much farther than Russia's natural borders and permeates the near abroad. To defend its homeland, Russia believes in creating a buffer zone to expand its borders and protect the Russian diaspora. Furthermore, NATO enlargement activities will only decrease Russia's buffer zone and continue to strain relations between Russia and the West. The entrance of Georgia and Ukraine into NATO exacerbates this problem.

Tempering Russia's behavior and influencing its foreign policy will continue to present future challenges to the United States, but Russia can be a potential strategic partner. Across the DIME spectrum, using a more diplomatic and economic approach by the United States has had an influence on Russia and should be patiently pursued. The military element of national power should be used with particular care. At the extreme end of the spectrum, military escalation and conventional warfare should be discouraged as it may lead to full-scale warfare and perhaps nuclear escalation. Placing missile defense assets back into Europe will likely be matched by Russia and incite an effective Russian A2/AD shield over the Baltic

States.[94] The military option should be nuanced and used indirectly to influence Russia's foreign policy. Military reassurance efforts that strengthen NATO partners and stabilize non-NATO member states' borders can neutralize Russia's use of ambiguous warfare. The appropriate integration of the U.S. and Western instruments of power, coupled with an understanding of Putin and Russian social and historic aspects, can further interests of the United States and its allies. Application of these factors can lead to an acceptable strategic partnership with Russia in the future. While all aspects of an acceptable approach to Russia merit exploration and analysis, the remainder of this monograph focuses almost entirely on the military element, with an emphasis on ways to achieve a balanced military response that effectively deters Russian aggression toward NATO and assures allies.

ENDNOTES - CHAPTER 1

1. Lauren Witlin, "Of Note: Mirror-Imaging and Its Dangers," *SAIS Review of International Affairs*, Vol. 28, No. 1, Winter-Spring 2000, pp. 09-90, available from *https://muse.jhu.edu/article/233105*, accessed January 16, 2016.

2. Ruth Deyermond, "Assessing the Reset: successes and failures in the Obama Administration's Russia policy, 2009–2012," *European Security*, Vol. 22, Iss. 4, available from *dx.doi.org/10.1080/09662839.2013.777704*, accessed December 31, 2015, p. 504

3. Sun Tzu, trans. by Samuel Griffith, *The Art of War*, New York: Oxford University Press, 1963, p. 84.

4. Summation of the perceptions of this monograph's authors from the research discussions with North Atlantic Treaty Organization (NATO), Supreme Headquarters Allied Powers Europe (SHAPE), U.S. Army Europe (USAEUR), and U.S. European Command (EUCOM), November 3-6, 2015.

5. Paul Starobin, "The Accidental Autocrat," *The Atlantic,* March 2005, available from *www.theatlantic.com/magazine/archive/2005/03/the-accidental-autocrat/303725/*, accessed January 16, 2016.

6. Robert Coalson, "Russia: Why The Chekist Mind-Set Matters," Radio Free Europe Radio Liberty, October 15, 2007, available from *www.rferl.org/content/article/1078954.html*, accessed March 18, 2016.

7. Bobo Lo, *Vladimir Putin and the Evolution of Russian Foreign Policy,* London, UK: Blackwell Publishing, 2003, p. 17.

8. *Ibid.*, p. 16.

9. Stefan Hedlund, "Economic Reform Under Putin 2.0: Will Petrodollars Suffice to Keep the Ship Afloat?" in Stephen J. Blank, ed., *Politics and Economics in Putin's Russia*, Carlisle Barracks, PA: Strategic Studies Institute and United States Army War College Press, 2013, p. 76.

10. Vladimir Vladimirovich Putin, Nataliya Gevorkyan, Natalya Timakova, Andrei V. Kolesnikov, and Catherine A. Fitzpatrick, *First Person: An Astonishingly Frank Self-portrait by Russia's President Vladimir Putin,* New York: Public Affairs, 2000, p. 142.

11. Boris Kagarlitsky, *Russia under Yeltsin and Putin: Neoliberal Autocracy,* London, UK: Pluto Press, 2002, p. 3.

12. Lo, p. 10.

13. Alexander Sokolowski, "Institutional Determinants of Chronic Policy Failure in Yeltsin's Russia," *Demokratizatsiya* Vol. 11, No. 3, Summer 2003, p. 412, available from *search.proquest.com.usawc.idm.oclc.org/docview/237202586?accountid=4444*, accessed March 17, 2016.

14. Lo, p. 1.

15. *Ibid.*, p. 4.

16. Olga Kryshtanovskaya and Stephen White, "Putin's Militocracy," *Post Soviet Affairs,* Vol. 19, No. 4, 2003, p. 291, available from *dx.doi.org/10.2747/1060-586X.19.4.289,* accessed March 17, 2016.

17. Lo, p. 17.

18. Daniel Beer, "Russia's Managed Democracy," *History Today,* Vol. 59, No. 5, May 2009, pp. 37-39, available from *search.proquest.com/docview/202818171?accountid=4444,* accessed March 1, 2016.

19. Marcel de Haas, "Medvedev's Security Policy: A Provisional Assessment," *Russian Analytical Digest,* Vol. 62, Iss. 9, June 18, 2009, p. 5, available from *www.css.ethz.ch/publications/pdfs/RAD-62.pdf,* accessed December 21, 2015.

20. *Ibid.,* p. 3. Note: the term "near abroad" is a commonly accepted reference to now independent countries which were once republics of the former Soviet Union. See Robert Kagan, "New Europe, Old Russia," *The Washington Post,* February 6, 2008, available from *www.washingtonpost.com/wp-dyn/content/article/2008/02/05/AR2008020502879.html,* accessed April 1, 2016.

21. de Haas, p. 5.

22. Henning Schroder, "Russia's National Security Strategy to 2020," *Russian Analytical Digest*, Vol. 62, Iss. 9, June 18, 2009, p. 10, available from *www.css.ethz.ch/publications/pdfs/RAD-62.pdf,* accessed December 21, 2015.

23. *Ibid.,* p. 6.

24. Anne Applebaum, "Putinism: The Ideology," LSE Ideas, Strategic Update 13.2, London, UK: The London School of Economics and Political Science, February 2013, p. 7.

25. Schroder, p. 10.

26. Applebaum, pp. 7-8.

27. *Ibid.,* p. 2.

28. Kryshtanovskaya and White, p. 301.

29. Ironically, the Duma is named after the Russian verb, *dymat*, which means, "to think."

30. Olga Oliker, Keith Crane, Lowell H. Schwartz, and Catherine Yusupov, *Russian Foreign Policy: Sources and Implications*, Arlington, VA: RAND, 2009, p. 12.

31. *Ibid.*

32. Arch Puddington, "Freedom in the World 2015, Discarding Democracy: Return to the Iron Fist," Freedom House Report, available from *https://freedomhouse.org/report/freedom-world/freedom-world-2015#.VprsKVMrJPM*, accessed January 16, 2016.

33. Applebaum, p. 6.

34. *Ibid.*, p. 2.

35. *Ibid.*, p. 6.

36. Vladimir Putin, "Annexation of Crimea speech," March 18, 2014, available from *en.kremlin.ru/events/president/news/20603*, accessed February 29, 2016.

37. Applebaum, p. 2.

38. *Ibid.*, p. 3.

39. Vladimir Putin, "The World Order: New Rules or a Game without Rules," Lecture, Meeting of the Valdai International Discussion Club in Sochi, Russia, October 24, 2014.

40. de Haas, p. 3.

41. Maureen Laurele, "The 'Russian World:' Russia's Soft Power and Geopolitical Imagination," Center on Global Interests Report, May 21, 2015, p. 7 available from *globalinterests.org/wp-content/uploads/2015/05/FINAL-CGI_Russian-World_Marlene-Laruelle.pdf*, accessed March 17, 2016.

42. The United States Special Operations Command White Paper that introduced the concept that defines gray zone challenges as "competitive interactions among and within state and non-state actors that fall between the traditional war and peace duality." As previously noted, this monograph will refer to such challenges and threats as ambiguous.

43. United States Department of the Army, *Training Circular (TC) 7-100, Hybrid Threat*, Washington, DC: United States Department of the Army, 2010, p. 1-1. It defines a hybrid threat as "the diverse and dynamic combination of regular forces, irregular forces, and/or criminal elements all unified to achieve mutually benefitting effects." Russia has used such threats as part of its ambiguous approach. To more holistically capture the essence of Russia's strategy, in that it used hybrid warfare and other actions in an umbrella of ambiguity, this monograph will use the terms "ambiguous threats" and "ambiguous warfare" and "ambiguous approach" in lieu of "hybrid threat" and "hybrid warfare" to underscore the difficulty of dealing with such threats emanating from Russia.

44. de Haas, p. 3.

45. *Ibid.*, p. 4.

46. Doug Mastriano *et al., Project 1704: A United States Army War College Analysis of Russian Strategy in Eastern Europe, and Appropriate U.S. Response and the Implications for U.S. Landpower*, Carlisle Barracks, PA: United States Army War College, 2015, p. 21.

47. English translation of Dmitry Medvedev, "Russia's National Security Strategy to 2020," Russian Federation, May 2009, available from *rustrans.wikidot.com/russia-s-national-security-strategy-to-2020*, accessed December 21, 2015.

48. Nikolai Pishchev, "NATO Myths and Realities," *Krasnaya Zvezda*, January 5, 1997, available from *fas.org/man/nato/national/msg00006c.htm*, accessed March 18, 2016.

49. North Atlantic Treaty Organization, "Relations with Russia," available from *www.nato.int/cps/en/natolive/topics_50090.htm*, accessed December 12, 2015.

50. Michael C. Ryan, "A Second Chance to Miss the Same Opportunity: Post-Putin and the Potential Re-Emergence of a More Reasonable Russia," *American Foreign Policy Interests*, Vol. 37, No. 3, 2015, p. 150.

51. *Ibid.*, p. 151.

52. Robert D. Kaplan, "Countering Putin's Grand Strategy," *Wall Street Journal*, February 12, 2015, *search.proquest.com.usawc.idm.oclc.org/docview/1654552152*, accessed January 14, 2016.

53. Ryan, p. 149.

54. S.R. Covington, *Putin's Choice for Russia*, Cambridge, MA: Harvard Kennedy School Belfer Center for Science and International Affairs, 2015, p. 3.

55. Mastriano *et al.*, p. 77.

56. Elbridge Colby and Jonathan Solomon, "Facing Russia: Conventional Defence and Deterrence in Europe," *Survival*, Vol. 56, Iss. 6, November 2015, p. 23, *www-tandfonline-com.usawc.idm.oclc.org/doi/abs/10.1080/00396338.2015.1116146*, accessed November 30, 2015.

57. Information derived from research discussions with Special Operations Command Europe (SOCEUR) staffers conducted by the author on November 4, 2015.

58. Nathan Friesel, "Hybrid Warfare; Four Challenges," lecture to the Defense Advanced Research Projects Agency (DARPA) offsite conference, Carlisle Barracks, PA: United States Army War College, December 2, 2015.

59. The North Atlantic Council (NAC), comprised of representatives of each NATO member states, is the alliance's highest decision-making authority.

60. Information derived from research discussions with NATO International staff for policy member and a NATO staff officer on November 3 and 4, 2015.

61. Colby and Solomon, p. 23.

62. Julie Ioffe, "Exclusive: The Pentagon Is Preparing New War Plans for a Baltic Battle Against Russia" *Foreign Policy*, September 18, 2015, available from *foreignpolicy.com.usawc.idm.oclc.org/2015/09/18/exclusive-the-pentagon-is-preparing-new-war-plans-for-a-baltic-battle-against-russia/*, accessed January 3, 2016.

63. de Haas, p. 3.

64. Putin, "The World Order: New Rules or a Game without Rules."

65. Aleksandr Korolkov, "Out of the blue: Khrushchev's 'Gift on a Golden Dish'," *Russia Beyond the Headlines*, supplement to *The Telegraph*, April 1, 2014, available from *https://issuu.com/rbth/docs/2014_03_dt_all?viewMode=magazine&e=1589469/7315023*, accessed on April 24, 2016.

66. Dave Johnson, *Russia's Approach to Conflict — Implications for NATO's Deterrence and Defence*, Research Paper No. 111, April 2015, Rome, Italy: NATO Defense College, p. 2, available from *www.ndc.nato.int/news/news.php?icode=797*, accessed November 28, 2015.

67. *Ibid.*, p. 12.

68. Covington, p. 6.

69. Douglas Mastriano, "Defeating Putin's Strategy of Ambiguity," War on the Rocks website, November 6, 2014, available from *warontherocks.com/2014/11/defeating-putins-strategy-of-ambiguity/*, accessed January 15, 2016.

70. Conflict: Protracted, Gray Zone, Ambiguous, and Hybrid Modes of War," in Dakota L. Wood ed., *2016 Index of U.S. Military Strength: Assessing America's Ability to Provide for the Common Defense*, Washington, DC: The Heritage Foundation, 2015, p. 26.

71. It should be noted that not all NATO allies see the Russia threat equally. There is a clear east-west divide: eastern NATO members perceive Russia as a significant threat, and the western

NATO members do not. Some European NATO members are afraid and feel the Alliance has an obligation to defend them—this inlcudes the Baltic States and some in allies Eastern Europe. This is in part due to the reality of Russian actions that demonstrate its willingness to use force (e.g., Ukraine), particularly when it perceives a risk to the Russian diaspora. Since some NATO members have significant populations of Russian diaspora, it is critical for the Alliance to be able to deter Russian agrression, but also for those NATO members with Russian diaspora to fully integrate them into society. This varying view on the Russian threat will create challenges for NATO to develop a common understanding of the threat and a commonly agreed response.

72. Heather A. Conley, "Putin's Europe," in Craig Cohan and Melissa G. Dalton eds., *2016 Global Forecast*, Washington, DC: Center for Strategic and International Studies, 2015, p. 39, available from *csis.org/files/publication/151116_Cohen_GlobalFore cast2016_Web.pdf*, accessed November 28, 2015.

73. *Ibid.*, p. 39.

74. Kaplan. He highlights Russia's use of such tools as buying media in Europe through third parties, criminality, bribing local politicians, and leveraging European dependence on Russian energy.

75. Doug Mastriano *et al.*, p. 47.

76. Deyermond, p. 500.

77. Vojtech Mastny, "How Able Was 'Able Archer'?: Nuclear Trigger and Intelligence in Perspective," *Journal of Cold War Studies*, Winter 2009, Vol. 11, No. 1, p. 108.

78. Deyermond, p. 518.

79. Celeste A. Wallander, Special Assistant to the President and Senior Director for Russia and Central Asia, National Security Council, "U.S. Policy on Russia," Washington, DC: CNAS Annual Conference, June 26, 2015.

80. *Ibid.*

81. *Ibid.*

82. GEN Philip M. Breedlove, *United States European Command Theater Strategy*, United States European Command, Headquarters, October 2015, p. 4, available from *www.eucom.mil/*, accessed February 6, 2016.

83. From "IR Paradigms, Approaches and Theories" The IR Theory Knowledge Base website, available from *www.irtheory.com/know.htm*, accessed November 30, 2015:

> A security dilemma refers to a situation wherein two or more states are drawn into conflict, possibly even war, over security concerns, even though none of the states actually desire conflict. Essentially, the security dilemma occurs when two or more states each feel insecure in relation to other states. None of the states involved want relations to deteriorate, let alone for war to be declared, but as each state acts militarily or diplomatically to make itself more secure, the other states interpret its actions as threatening. An ironic cycle of unintended provocations emerges, resulting in an escalation of the conflict which may eventually lead to open warfare.

84. Colby and Solomon, p. 21.

85. *Ibid.*, p. 42.

86. Covington, p. 21.

87. Schroder, p. 10.

88. Putin, "The World Order: New Rules or a Game without Rules."

89. Peter Baker and Steven Erlanger, "Russia Uses Money and Ideology to Fight Western Sanctions," *The New York Times*, June 7, 2015.

90. Meeting with AMB. Steven Pifer of the Brookings Institution, January 6, 2016, cited with permission by Mr. Pifer.

91. Edward Christie, "Sanctions after Crimea: Have they worked?" *NATO Review Magazine,* 2015, available from *www.nato.int/docu/Review/2015/Russia/sanctions-after-crimea-have-they-worked/EN/index.htm,* accessed March 18, 2016.

92. Rebecca M. Nelson, "U.S. Sanctions on Russia: Economic Implications," *Current Politics and Economics of Russia, Eastern and Central Europe,* Vol. 30, No. 1, 2015, p. 201, available from *search.proquest.com.usawc.idm.oclc.org/docview/1770385425?account id=4444,* accessed March 16, 2016.

93. European Parliament briefing, "Economic impact on the EU of sanctions over Ukraine conflict," October 2015, available from *www.europarl.europa.eu/RegData/etudes/BRIE/2015/569020/EPRS_BRI(2015)569020_EN.pdf,* accessed January 18, 2016.

94. Vladimir Putin, "Being Strong: Why Russia needs to rebuild its military." *Foreign Policy,* February 21, 2012, available from *foreignpolicy.com/2012/02/21/being-strong/,* accessed February 29, 2016.

CHAPTER 2

DETERRENCE STRATEGIES IN AN INCREASINGLY COMPLEX EUROPEAN SECURITY ENVIRONMENT

Europe is approaching an inflection point where decisions to follow either the instinct for collective interests or individual interests could transform that region into a very dangerous operational theater.
—General Martin Dempsey[1]

We cannot be fully certain of what Russia will do next. We still cannot fully discern Mr. Putin's intent. But I can observe the capabilities and capacities that Russia is creating across our [area of operations]. And I continue [to] believe that we must strengthen our deterrence and that EUCOM and our NATO allies must continue to adapt by improving our readiness and responsiveness.
—General Philip M. Breedlove[2]

How to deter Russia effectively, without provoking conflict, is a subject of prolonged debate, complicated by the challenge of defining what deterrence is and how to do it in today's security context. The United States' and North Atlantic Treaty Organization's (NATO's) primary challenge is deterring both a conventional threat and an ambiguous threat as Russia works toward achieving its objectives. In his 2016-posture statement before Congress, the then U.S. European Command (EUCOM) Commander, General Philip Breedlove, speaking of Operation ATLANTIC RESOLVE stated that:

Now that we are nearly two years into this operation, our efforts are adding a deterrence component with the goal of deterring Russia from any further aggressive actions.[3]

However, what is not entirely clear is how such efforts, as well as others, are contributing to deterrence. It is therefore essential to understand what deterrence is, the calculus underlying decisions regarding deterrence options, and the effects that such decisions might have on the actors. A baseline theoretical and definitional exploration of deterrence and a subsequent assessment of current U.S. efforts to deter Russia will demonstrate that the U.S.' ability to deter Russian aggression using conventional forces is difficult, although not impossible. Solutions to mitigate these challenges will follow this brief discussion, focusing on ways to deter Russia's potential use of conventional forces as well as its use of ambiguous warfare.

THEORETICAL AND DEFINITIONAL FOUNDATIONS OF DETERRENCE

Since war is not an act of senseless passion but is controlled by its political object, the value of this object must determine the sacrifices to be made for it in magnitude and also duration.[4]

Clausewitz's calculus applies to deterrence as well as war. The bulk of deterrence theory evolved during the Cold War when the United States and its NATO allies faced the Soviet Union and the Warsaw Pact. Cold War deterrence relied heavily on nuclear weapons, but shifted to include conventional deterrence as the Soviet Union developed its own strategic nuclear deterrent capabilities.[5]

Soldiers from Charlie Company, 2nd Battalion, 8th Cavalry Regiment, 1st Brigade Combat Team, 1st Cavalry Division fire rounds from their M1A2 Abrams Tanks at the Adazi Training Area, Latvia, on November 6, 2014. These activities were part of the U.S. Army Europe-led Operation ATLANTIC RESOLVE land force assurance training taking place across Estonia, Latvia, Lithuania, and Poland to enhance multinational interoperability, strengthen relationships among allied militaries, contribute to regional stability, and demonstrate U.S. commitment to NATO.

Figure 2-1. Operation ATLANTIC RESOLVE.

With the end of the Cold War, the focus on deterrence diminished as the threats against the United States became increasingly impotent.[6] Nevertheless, nuclear deterrence retains a role, a point that Secretary of Defense Ashton Carter underscored in a recent speech at the Reagan National Defense Forum.[7] Yet, in the context of today's security environment, the threat of large-scale nuclear attack or the use of tactical nuclear weapons between the United States/NATO and Russia seems unlikely. Contemporary discussions include new aspects such as how to deter an ambiguous threat where attribution is elusive. The challenge in today's security environment is, therefore, twofold. It includes deterrence against a conventional force of another state actor, and deterrence against ambiguous threats, whether those emanate from state or non-state actors.[8]

The underlying premise of deterrence is one actor, the deterring force, influencing the decision-making calculus of another in such a manner that the decisions made are to the benefit of the deterring force. Thomas Schelling, one of the fathers of classical deterrence theory, notes that deterrence includes the threat of the use of force, and the harm it would inflict, with the aim to influence behavior.[9] Daniel Byman and Matthew Waxman also highlight deterrence's role in influencing behavior.[10] John Mearsheimer noted that deterrence focuses on the deterring force persuading an adversary not to act by getting him to perceive that the costs and risks outweigh the benefits.[11] Gordon Craig and Alexander George arrive at similar conclusions.[12] While approaches to deterrence vary, there are common elements among them, credibility and capability, as key tenants to effective deterence; and a cost-benefit calculus that influences behavior.

Robert A. Pape defines two fundamental types of deterrence: by punishment and by denial. Punishment focuses primarily on raising the costs or risks associated with the adversary's potential actions. In line with Pape's definition, Austin Long from the RAND Corporation defines deterrence by punishment as the threat of inflicting harm on the opponent to the degree that he would calculate any provocation as not cost beneficial.[13] Deterrence by denial, according to Pape, prevents the adversary from achieving its political or military objectives, thus reducing the benefits.[14] Similarly, Long defines deterrence by denial as defending interests to prevent opponent access to them.[15]

In order to be effective, a deterring force must be credible. Schelling notes that communicating intentions to the adversary is very difficult.[16] He states:

> we go to great lengths to tell the Russians that they will have America to contend with if they. . . attack countries associated with us. Saying so does not always make it believed.[17]

Herein lies an extremely complex challenge for the deterring force. Many factors influence credibility, including: political will and resolution; domestic pressures; economic and budget constraints; and force capability and disposition, such as size, posture, and readiness. According to Craig and George, credibility consists of two elements. The first is the deterring force's ability to convince its opponent that it has the will and resolution to do what it threatens to do, and that it will back its commitments to respond to attacks on its interests. The second element of credibility requires possessing the capabilities to do what one says one is going to do. Thus, the deterring force's threats must be both credible and sufficiently potent that the costs and risks to the adversary of attacking outweigh the benefits.[18] Byman and Waxman note that an adversary's perception of the strength of the deterring force will largely influence its decisions.[19] Thus, the capability of the deterring force, both actual and perceived, underpins the deterring force's credibility. Highlighting the significance of a capable force, Craig and George note that deterrence fails when the force applied is either inappropriate or unusable.[20] Therefore, the right capability is critical when attempting to deter a threat.

Understanding the threat and the adversary's intentions are contributing factors in determining the right capability. Multiple factors, aside from the adversary's force size and strength, contribute to the deterring force's calculus, such as the adversary's intent and political will, among others.

It is even more difficult to determine what capabilities to apply against an ambiguous threat, particularly when applying conventional forces against those threats is not viable. Deterring an ambiguous threat may require a set of different capabilities than those used to deter a conventional threat. These capabilities include a greater reliance on the other instruments of national power. Craig and George highlight that actors rarely apply deterrence options in isolation and include other diplomatic strategies as part of the deterrence calculus.[21] Mearsheimer further highlights that policy decisions on deterrence must consider all the resources at one's disposal and consider the second and third order effects.[22]

The credibility and capability behind a deterrence force influence an adversary's cost-benefit calculus. Byman and Waxman use a cost-benefit model in which they identify basic elements that are helpful in understanding the cost-benefit relationship inherent in deterrence. First, benefits are the value the adversary derives from an action, which are ultimately difficult for the deterring force to determine or influence. Second, costs define the price an adversary anticipates paying in pursuit of a particular action. This includes the cost to continue resistance versus the cost to comply with the coercer. The final element is the probability of achieving the benefits or suffering the costs. This is very subjective in nature and a function of the deterring force's credibility and capability, both as he perceives it and as the adversary perceives it.[23] Pape provides further fidelity on the cost-benefit relationship by using what he terms "the logic of coercion."[24] Pape defines the logic of coercion, from an adversary's perspective, wherein the adversary calculates the hope of attaining any benefits outweigh the potential costs. In such a case, the adversary concedes.[25] Pape uses the following equation to define the logic of coercion:

$$R = B\, p(B) - C\, p(C),$$

where:

	R	= value of resistance
	B	= potential benefits of resistance
	p(B)	= probability of attaining benefits by continued resistance
	C	= potential costs of resistance
	p(C)	= probability of suffering costs

Figure 2-2. Logic of Coercion.[26]

The cost-benefit model of course has it limits, particularly since much of the decision-making on both sides is based on perceptions and probability, not to mention the challenges of quantifying deterrence. Nor can it account for the human dimension of decision-making. Nevertheless, it provides a baseline from which to assess options for deterrence.

ASSESSING DETERRENCE

Assessing the effects of deterrence activities, and how to make necessary adjustments, is not easy in a complex security environment. During the Cold War, although force posture fluctuated, the numbers and locations of U.S. and NATO forces, as well as the robust nuclear capabilities, easily defined what deterrence looked like.[27] Arguably, this approach worked since the Soviet Union never attacked, and ultimately ceded when the costs became too high. The landscape, in terms of force size and presence, has completely changed since the end of the Cold War for both NATO and Russia. There are currently no U.S. Corps or Divisions stationed in Europe, and the viability of NATO to provide ready and capable equivalent units is questionable. The United States has drawn down its maneuver forces in Europe to two brigade combat teams (one Stryker Brigade Combat Team (SBCT) and one Airborne Infantry Brigade Combat Team (ABCT)), and limited enabling capabilities (e.g. no bridging assets capable of supporting an M1 tank, and significant reductions in the size of the aviation brigade). Due to their force reductions, European NATO allies are limited in their capability to organize and deploy large forces and to move them rapidly across borders in the event of an emerging crisis. Further, NATO has limited forces along its eastern flank—mostly just national forces resident within each NATO member's territory. It would prove challenging for the United States to move forces quickly enough to preclude a fait accompli, a point further addressed in an another chapter in this monograph. Russia has also reduced its force strength from Cold War levels, but it still maintains 27 motorized brigades, 4 airborne divisions, and 1 tank army. In quantitative terms, Russia has numerical superiority in tanks and artillery pieces, and roughly equivalent numbers of infantry fighting vehicles and armored personnel carriers as the United States.[28] On the other hand, RAND notes that Russia can position 22 battalions on its western border (roughly 7 brigades),[29] and arguably more if the conflict in Ukraine were to subside or turn cold. Russia also has the advantage of interior lines of communication and the ability to muster quickly and move forces, as evidenced by its snap exercises. One must, therefore, wonder whether the United States and NATO actually pose a credible and capable deterrent force in Europe. In order to answer that question, it is first necessary to understand two things. What are Russia's objectives and intentions? What threats are the United States and NATO deterring?

As addressed in Chapter 1 and supported by a recent U.S. Army War College analysis of Russian strategy in Eastern Europe, Russia seeks to maintain its influence over its near abroad, and to discredit NATO.[30] This is also consistent with the assessment of various headquarters within Europe, including NATO, Supreme Headquarters Allied Powers Europe (SHAPE), EUCOM, and U.S. Army Europe (USAREUR). NATO's center of gravity—its most important source of strength—is Alliance cohesion; and Russia's actions seek to fracture that cohesion.[31] Deputy Secretary of Defense Robert Work echoed this assessment in a recent speech at the Royal United Services Institute (RUSI) in London.[32] Elbridge Colby and Jonathan Solomon similarly refer to Russia's attempt to recreate its sphere of influence and to break the cohesion of the Alliance.[33] Kaplan refers to this risk to NATO by highlighting the fact that NATO does not, "protect its members against Russian subversion from within."[34] Fractures already exist as evidenced by the varying degrees to which the NATO members perceive Russia as a threat.[35] Therefore, it is possible to surmise that Russia's objectives include increasing its influence in Europe, by stopping NATO and European Union (EU) enlargement and influence; and it intends to exploit fractures in the Alliance. As noted in Chapter 1, in pursuit of this objective, Russia has demonstrated its willingness to use its conventional land forces (albeit not always overtly), as well as other capabilities. For example, Russia used cyberattacks on Estonia in 2007, and again during the Georgia and Ukraine conflicts to advance its objectives.[36]

Russia's use of ambiguous warfare, as previously referenced in the Center for Strategic and International Studies' *2016 Global Forecast*,[37] coupled with its use of conventional forces, demonstrates Moscow's approach to achieving its objectives. The U.S. Army War College analysis of Russian strategy in Eastern Europe drew three key conclusions about Russia's approach to achieving its objectives. First, Russia relies heavily on landpower, particularly in its near abroad. Second, it uses airborne and special operations forces (SOF) in both conventional and non-conventional roles. Finally, Russia effectively uses information operations (and to this one could add cyber) to influence the strategic narrative. Therefore, the United States and NATO must be capable of countering all three of these elements: Russian land forces; SOF, particularly when used in an ambiguous role; and information operations, which are often employed using ambiguous warfare.

Assessing the credibility and capability of the United States and NATO to deter these threats is open to a wide range of subjective analysis. Credibility includes the will and resolution to defend one's interests.[38] The United States has repeatedly emphasized its commitment to defend the Baltic States and Eastern Europe, and any other NATO member, against aggression. In a September 2014 speech delivered in Estonia, President Barack Obama confirmed the U.S.' commitment to defending NATO allies and their territorial integrity.[39] Secretary of Defense Ashton Carter reinforced the President's comments by noting that NATO remains a cornerstone to maintaining international order and underscored the significance of the Article 5 commitment.[40] NATO has yet to be openly tested in an Article 5 scenario against Russia, nor should it want to be in a position to consider invoking an Article 5. Nevertheless, NATO is making significant strides to enhance its credibility via various capabilities agreed at the 2014 Wales Summit, such as the Very High Readiness Joint Task Force (VJTF), which was recently validated in an exercise in 2015. NATO is expected to further enhance its efforts at the upcoming 2016 Warsaw Summit, with a focus on its deterrence and defense posture. Despite all these efforts, Russia's use of ambiguous warfare is a way to avoid testing the U.S. or NATO resolve, while still progressing toward achieving its objective to fracture the Alliance.

That said, the United States is making steps to demonstrate its commitment to Article 5. For example, the United States announced the European Reassurance Initiative (ERI) in June 2014 to provide funding for, among other things, increased exercises, deployments, and activities focused on building partner capacity.[41] Since ERI's announcement, the United States has increased the number of exercises and is vigorously conducting bilateral and multilateral training events across NATO, with a focus on the Baltic States and Eastern Europe, under the auspices of Operation ATLANTIC RESOLVE.[42] It also includes a renewed emphasis on NATO operationalizing its Readiness Action Plan (RAP).[43] However, increasing the quantity of exercises and training does not necessarily equate to credibility. Planners should design exercises and training to focus on specific capability objectives, and to demonstrate critical capabilities that might be used in support of Article 5. Further, such efforts should include a deliberate supporting public affairs and information operations plan (further explored later in this monograph), all of which contributes to increasing credibility, or at least the perception thereof.

Source: *www.eucom.mil/media-library/photo/32982/allied-port-ops-in-riga-reinforce-operation-atlantic-resolve.*

Soldiers from the 3rd Infantry Division offload an M1A2 Abrams Main Battle Tank from the transportation vessel "Liberty Promise" March 9, 2015, the Riga Universal Terminal docks. More than 100 pieces of equipment, including the tanks, M2A3 Bradley Fighting Vehicles, and assorted military cargo, moved on to sites in other areas of Latvia as well as Estonia and Lithuania in support of Operation ATLANTIC RESOLVE.

Figure 2-3. Rotational Presense.

Returning to the two elements of credibility (will and capability), while the United States and the Alliance are making strides to demonstrate their collective will to use force, they must do more to develop the capabilities that underpin it. As previously noted, credibility is validated only when it is tested. While the goal is never to need to validate credibility, the United States and NATO should not rely solely on the ERI and other U.S.-centric activities, or NATO activities as part of the RAP, to demonstrate a credible unified Alliance commitment to collective defense. Nor do any of these activities readily equate to an Alliance capable of defending its borders from outside aggression. For credibility to be effective, the United States and the Alliance must also continue to develop capable forces in Europe in order to effectively deter Russia against both conventional and ambiguous threats. The NATO Defense Planning Process is a critical tool in developing these capabilities.[44] Yet NATO may need to revise how it conducts its defense planning, for example by better tying the necessary capabilities to the identified threats.[45]

An outdated NATO Strategic Concept, NATO's baseline strategy document, also hinders NATO's credibility. This document clearly sees Russia as a cooperative, albeit challenging, partner in European security.[46] The Alliance is holding on to this dated Strategic Concept despite the fact that the security environment, and Russia's role in it, have clearly changed since 2010. The main factor behind not changing the Strategic Concept is a reluctance by the United States to move forward with any changes in light of an impending change in administration.[47] Despite this delay in adopting an updated Alliance strategy, efforts to increase capability and capacity through the ERI, Operation ATLANTIC RESOLVE, and RAP activities, continue.

NATO faces other challenges to providing a capable deterrent force in Europe, including reversing two decades of declining defense budgets. Defense spending by European NATO members has declined by 28 percent since 1990, which is in part normal given the lack of an existential, ideologically driven context present during the Cold War.[48] These reductions and a widespread move toward professionalized militaries have led to a significantly smaller European force structure. This coupled with a focus on expeditionary operations over the last decade and the economic crisis of the last several years, have led to a European force that is less capable across the entire spectrum of conflict and that struggles to field a corps, and, in many instances, a division.[49] The result is a significant decrease in military capabilities available to defend against threats across an enlarged Alliance flank.[50] However, it appears the downward trend in defense spending may be reversing. In his annual report, NATO Secretary General Jens Stoltenberg noted that European allies defense cuts have essentially stopped. He noted, that more needs to be done to increase defense investments in light of emerging security challenges, such as Russia.[51] Russia, despite a decade of deterioration of its armed forces, has progressively increased its defense budget since 2000, and focused on modernization. For example, from the period between 2007 and 2015, Russia increased its defense spending from an estimated $37 billion to just over $53 billion, an almost 70 percent increase.[52]

One way to measure capability is to assess expert opinion. According to three-quarters of the National Journal's Security Insiders, NATO does not have the capabilities to counter Russia.[53] Those who disagreed did caveat their opinions with insistence that the Alliance needs to make adjustments.[54]

Another way of measuring capability is through war games and simulations. Two recent studies indicate that, taking into account the current U.S. force posture in Europe as well as European NATO members' capabilities, the Alliance would not be able to defend the Baltic States against a Russia invasion, regardless of the likelihood of such a scenario. In a report prepared for the National Commission on the Future of the Army,[55] the Burke-Macgregor Group LLC, concluded the United States could not defeat a Russian ground invasion in the Baltic States.[56] RAND similarly concluded that NATO cannot prevent a Russian invasion and occupation of the Baltic States.[57]

This assessment draws several conclusions. First, the United States and NATO backed up their commitment to collective defense with ERI, Operation ATLANTIC RESOLVE, NATO's recent adoption of its RAP, and an increased rotational presence of many allies in the Baltic States and Eastern Europe.[58] While these commitments and activities provide a reassuring effect to the Baltic States and Eastern Europe, they do not automatically provide a credible deterrence strategy. Further, Russia has yet to overtly test that credibility against NATO members. It is therefore unclear whether the costs to Russia have gone up or the ability of Russia to secure its objectives has gone down. This may lead Russia to believe it can continue its current approach. Finally, based on current force structure, NATO lacks the capability to defeat a surprise Russian conventional attack into the Baltic States or Eastern Europe, regardless of the likelihood of such a scenario.

Capability is the backbone of credibility, and that is something that the United States and NATO together can and should address to enhance deterrence against Russian aggression. To that end, the United States and NATO should address ways to enhance capabilities, and thus their credibility, so that it will provide a deterrent against Russian aggression and assist in addressing other security challenges as they emerge.

DERIVING STRATEGY OPTIONS

Charles F. Herman once stated that, "Shifts in values, environment, capabilities, or threats may lead to the need for altered strategies for minimizing the threats posed to our security."[59] Policymakers and strategists need to approach deterrence differently today than in the Cold War due to the character of the threat from Russia, the change in U.S. force posture in Europe, and a decreased Alliance capability to defend itself.

In today's world, Russia uses aggression in areas where its influence is already strong, its interests are historical (e.g. Crimea), and where it has the military advantage and can therefore achieve its objectives (e.g. Georgia and Ukraine). Its invasion of Georgia in 2008, illegal annexation of Crimea in 2014, and military involvement in Eastern Ukraine beginning that same year are cases where Russia's actions have created divisions within Europe. Russia continues to try to gain influence in the Baltic States and Eastern Europe, but it knows that the United States and European states, particularly those that are part of NATO, would not tolerate Russian overt use of force against a NATO ally.

Russia, therefore, uses ambiguous warfare to cause fissures within the European security institutions and increase its influence. Therefore, the United States and NATO must be prepared to deter against both conventional and ambiguous threats. Taking these points into consideration, it is possible to derive two strategies to achieve deterrence: deterrence by denial and deterrence by punishment.

Deterrence by Denial — Denying Access Through Presence.

Deterrence by denial focuses on denying the adversary its objectives. It seeks to deny Russia access to the Baltic States and Eastern Europe. Unlike during the Cold War, positioning multiple divisions with hundreds of thousands of soldiers along NATO's eastern flank is unlikely to be acceptable to the United States or most other NATO allies and could lead to a security dilemma with Russia. With that understanding, and noting current Alliance force posture and its ability to defend, a Russian advance into the Baltic States would likely happen quickly and come with minimal military cost to Russia. While the Alliance could not prevent a fait accompli, it can enhance its presence in the Baltic States and Eastern Europe to demonstrate its commitment to common defense.

A conventional attack would likely lead to NATO's invocation of Article 5, followed by a massive counteroffensive to repel the Russians from Alliance territory. Russia would therefore lose its ability to influence Europe, and instead of fracturing the Alliance, it could serve to galvanize NATO against Russia and stiffen the resolve of the threatened states to resist Russian pressure. The benefits derived from such a conventional military incursion into the Baltic States are thus reduced by Alliance presence. Second order effects could put the Russian regime at risk of collapse, thus further decreasing the benefits to the regime.

By decreasing the probability of Russia achieving its objectives to influence Europe and fracture the Alliance, the costs of such an attack would outweigh the benefits. The decreasing value of the object therefore increases the deterrent effect.

There are multiple ways for the United States and the Alliance to enhance their presence in the Baltic States and Eastern Europe that contribute to deterrence by denial. Deterrence by denial would involve continuing the rotational presence in the Baltic States and Central and Eastern Europe using ERI, Operation ATLANTIC RESOLVE, enhanced air policing, and RAP activities. Rotational forces would use the European Activity Set (EAS) along the Alliance's eastern flank. The U.S. Congress should also approve the President's 2017 budget proposal that includes funding to establish an ABCT set of Army Prepositioned Stock (APS) in Europe.[60] Joint and combined training and exercises with NATO forces should also continue.

Deterrence by denial is particularly enhanced as other European NATO members, Germany in particular, and possibly other partners, contribute to a regular rotational presence. Germany plans to begin rotations in 2016.[61] This would speak volumes in terms of Alliance commitment. These are all actions that U.S. and NATO allies can take in the immediate and short term with the effect of denying Russia its objectives. However, more must be done to effectively deter Russian aggression.

Deterrence by Punishment — A Delayed Counterattack.

While a continual presence, rotational forces, air policing, and robust training exercises are necessary, and demonstrate U.S. and Alliance commitment and will, it is clear that the United States and NATO just do not have enough forces to prevent Russia from invading and occupying all or part of the Baltic States, however unlikely that scenario might be.

U.S. Army M1A2 Abrams tanks arrive at the Grafenwoehr Training Area, Germany, January 31, 2014. The vehicles were part of the European Activity Set designed to support the U.S. Army's European Rotational Force and the NATO Response Force during training exercises and real-world missions.

Figure 2-4. European Activity Set.

A deterrence by punishment strategy focuses on developing a viable and potent capability for a delayed counterattack in the unlikely event of a Russian invasion. An underlying assumption of this approach is that the obligation established by Article 3 of the North Atlantic Treaty, that members defend themselves against an armed attack, has been ineffective or failed for one or more allies.[62] Therefore, the focus should be on building national capability within the Alliance to repel a Russian invasion and occupation of Alliance territory, if deterrence by denial fails. Not only would such a capability serve as a deterrent effect, it would also underpin the credibility of the United States and Alliance commitment to Article 5, and raise the costs and risks to Russia.

European NATO members need to enhance their capabilities if the Alliance is to get to the point at which it has the ability to deter Russian armed aggression with the threat of a massive counter-offensive. Budgets are tight, so this is not an easy task, nor is this an immediate solution. Developing the required national capabilities will take years, which underscores the necessity of the deterrence by denial approach previously addressed. This will serve as the primary means of deterrence against Russia while the United States and NATO re-focus efforts to develop requisite capabilities on the European continent. In developing these capabilities, the Alliance will also increase its ability to deny Russia its objectives, thus highlighting an interconnectedness between deterrence by denial and deterrence by punishment.

Developing Alliance Capabilities.

The United States has several mechanisms in place as part of its security cooperation activities, as well as those associated with ERI and Operation ATLANTIC RESOLVE, to focus efforts on enhancing and exercising Alliance capabilities. However, senior USAREUR officials admit that while they are indeed doing a lot to reassure allies, there is no coordinated effort on the intent, other than reassurance, behind these activities.[63] To remedy this problem, EUCOM and USAREUR need to better coordinate and streamline their activities to focus on enhancing and exercising Alliance capabilities. In particular, EUCOM and US-AREUR should more effectively make use of NATO capability targets—part of the NATO Defense Planning Process—to define the types of activities that will focus on lacking capabilities.

EUCOM should clearly define the approach in its Theater Campaign Plan (TCP) and associated Country-specific Security Cooperation Sections, and provide the resources USAREUR needs to achieve its defined objectives. This requires a persistent coordinated staff effort among EUCOM, USAREUR, SHAPE, NATO, and NATO's Land Component Command (LAND-COM) in Izmir, Turkey. These activities should ultimately support Phase 0 (shape) and Phase 1 (deter)[64] operations in support of EUCOM's TCP. However, it is not entirely clear there is a coherent Phase 0 and Phase 1 plan, or if they are included as part of draft contingency plans.[65] All this implies that the commands properly train their staff, particularly those involved in security cooperation, to conduct strategic and operational planning, and understand the nesting of national security objectives with Alliance capability targets.[66] A subsequent chapter to this monograph further elaborates on the issue of capability development, particularly with the use of exercises.

European NATO members must also do their part by progressively increasing their defense budgets and finding effective ways to increase capabilities. NATO has programs in place aimed toward that end, such as the Connected Forces Initiative,[67] but they are only as good as the allies' commitment to the programs. Some allies are also working independently toward increasing capabilities. For example, Germany announced in April 2015 that it is buying back 100 Leopard II tanks in order to increase its defense capabilities and provide flexible options.[68]

As the Alliance develops a more capable force—that underpins credibility—it will increase the perceived costs and the probability of such costs in the event of a Russian invasion into Alliance territory. These costs, as noted above, would come after such an invasion via a massive Alliance counterattack against Russia to restore Alliance territory. By raising the probability and degree of perceived costs, the perceived net benefits of a Russian invasion into Alliance territory go down. Therefore, this reduces the value of the object for Russia and increases the deterrent effect.

Deterrence by Denial—Denying the Ability to Fracture and Influence.

The capability development efforts associated with both of the above deterrence strategies focus purely on a conventional threat, and not on an ambiguous threat. A Russian conventional attack against the Alliance, while plausible, is unlikely. The more likely scenario is that Russia continues to use ambiguous warfare to fracture Alliance cohesion, and gain influence in Europe. Russia is opportunistic and is likely to leverage other events to further achieve its objectives. Case in point is the refugee crisis in Europe. Russia could use the crisis to find fracture points and exploit them, such as EU members' differing views on border security. One way to counter this ambiguous approach is to deter by denial—to deny Russia its objectives of increasing its influence in Europe and fracturing the Alliance through ambiguous warfare. Activities conducted under the first part of a denial strategy would help to deny Russia its objectives by enhancing Alliance cohesion.

There is also a vital second part to deterrence by denial. As previously noted, Russia is using ambiguous warfare to create fissures within Europe. This is a particularly challenging problem, since it is difficult to identify the activities, attribute the source, and determine what resources to pit against such activities. This effort has an important foreign internal defense (FID) element to it, and requires a strategy with more than just a military element. It should also include information, intelligence, law enforcement, economic, financial, and diplomatic instruments, among potentially others.

In many, if not most nations, the ability to counter Russian ambiguous warfare is largely a law enforcement function. It also has an economic and diplomatic element and significant information and intelligence instruments as well, particularly in light of the prevalence of cyberwarfare. Hence, the United States needs a concerted effort among interagency partners to identify those areas where Washington can assist European NATO members to develop capabilities to deter Russia's ambiguous warfare. This includes synchronizing the EUCOM Country-specific Security Cooperation Sections of its TCP with the U.S. Embassy Integrated Country Strategies, and finding synergies where possible. EUCOM has the structure to facilitate this process within the J-5 (Strategic Planning and Policy) and J-9 (Interagency Partnering) directorates, but it is unclear how much buy-in there is from both the Department of Defense (DoD) and interagency partners. This implies the need for EUCOM to work closely with country teams in U.S. embassies across Europe to clearly define approaches and synchronize efforts to help allies develop capabilities required to counter ambiguous threats. The U.S. military could add value to this process through the National Guard's State Partnership Program (SPP). This program has the flexibility to bring in state agencies and members of the National Guard with capabilities required to create synergies, thus, augmenting efforts of the interagency country team. Where critical national security objectives are at stake, the National Security Council should play a critical role in coordinating efforts among the interagency to define the risks and potential threats, and develop appropriate policies and strategies.

European NATO members also have a responsibility to work together, particularly those who are also EU members. Failure to work together could lead to fractures between and among states. Franklin D. Kramer *et al.*, posit that this requires a fourth core task for the Alliance that focuses on national resiliency against ambiguous threats. This "stability generation" seeks to enhance Alliance capacity to prevent and dissuade threats that seek to attack or influence society.[69] Many of the functions required to protect society reside within government agencies outside of the military, and cross over into the purview of the EU. These are the functions and associated capabilities (e.g. law enforcement, border control) that are essential to deter ambiguous threats. Since NATO does not possess or have influence over these types of capabilities, it implies the need for enhanced cooperation and coordination between NATO and the EU. In support, the U.S. DoD should also reconsider its representation at the U.S. Mission to the EU in order to enhance the ability to synchronize efforts with NATO and EUCOM.

These are all critical activities that will help to secure the Alliance's center of gravity — cohesion and unity — and deny Russia the ability to influence European security affairs. These efforts, by denying objectives, would decrease the probability of Russia obtaining the benefits of its action, thus decreasing the value of the object and increasing the deterrent effect. A subsequent chapter to this monograph further elaborates on this aspect of building partner capacity through theater security cooperation (TSC), especially including FID.

A NOTE REGARDING REASSURANCE

Historically, security assurances applied primarily to the use of nuclear weapons, both to prevent nuclear states from threatening other states, and to provide assistance to those states who become the victims of nuclear aggression.[70] Thus, security assurance includes providing a security umbrella with the protection of nuclear weapons. This was very much the case during the Cold War as well as in nuclear non-proliferation activities,[71] and which has been the topic of a great deal of research.[72] However, the security assurances sought by the Baltic States and Eastern Europe are less about the nuclear umbrella and non-proliferation and more about the Alliance's commitment to collective defense and response to Russian aggression. This is why, on June 3, 2014, President Obama announced the ERI.[73] As previously noted, the ERI, along with Operation ATLANTIC RESOLVE, are critical components of building national capabilities that in the end, make allies security contributors. Based on the warm welcome from local communities to an increased U.S. presence in the Baltic States and Eastern Europe,[74] one can assume that the level of reassurance has indeed increased, despite the call from some allies for more presence. Yet, reassurance will only become viable and credible as all Alliance members improve and develop capabilities that provide the Alliance with the full set of forces and capabilities it requires[75] to legitimately deter Russian aggression.

Ultimately, in the case of Russian aggression, assurances of an Allied and U.S. response will depend on, among other things, the strategic context, the attribution of ambiguous threats, the scale of the aggression, and the national interests impacted. It is difficult to state definitively how the Alliance, and particularly the United States, would respond to what the Baltic States or Eastern Europe might see as Russian aggression if the methods are ambiguous or attribution is difficult. This is where building national resiliency capabilities is critical.

Efforts to arrive at a political decision and efforts to deploy forces may indeed take time. Yet two cautions are in order. First, the United States and NATO cannot afford to reassure allies to the point where they solely rely on the United States or NATO writ large, to ensure their security. This could leave the Alliance in a deficit of capabilities (the assured ally being a consumer of security and not a producer). It could also leave the assured ally vulnerable to adversarial actions that fall below the threshold of an Article 5 incident and against which it can neither defend nor respond. Reassurance activities must therefore seek to assure allies that the Alliance will respond to its collective defense commitments, while at the same time assisting that Ally to develop its own capabilities. This is consistent with Kramer *et al.*'s approach to resiliency.[76]

Second, the United States and NATO must be careful that its reassurance activities do not provoke further Russian aggression, or lead to a new security dilemma. Indicators point to Russian military responses to increased U.S. and NATO activities along Russia's western border. For example, at the same time Operation DRAGOON RIDE was taking place, Russia doubled its troop levels from 40,000 to 80,000 for mass exercises across Russia.[77] The challenge, according to Arnold Wolfers, is convincing each other that the accumulation of power is not intended for offensive operations against the other.[78] This is, therefore, a delicate balancing game. It must take into consideration Russian actions in Georgia and Ukraine, but also understand Russian intentions and the likelihood of a conventional attack—balanced against the reality of potential ambiguous activities and Russian influence in Europe. Any strategy toward Russia therefore requires continual assessment and adjustment, and a well-coordinated and thought-out public affairs and information operations plan.

Source: U.S. Army photo by Capt. Spencer Garrison, *https://www.flickr.com/photos/usarmyeurope_images/*.

In the fall of 2015, the U.S. Army's 2nd Cavalry Regiment completed an 800 km military movement across Germany, Czech Republic, Slovak Republic, and Hungary, to demonstrate continued commitment and cooperation between NATO allies and to exercise freedom of movement across Europe. Along the way, U.S. Soldiers from 4th Squadron, 2nd Cavalry Regiment received logistical support from their allies in the host nations' militaries.

Figure 2-5. OPERATION DRAGOON RIDE.

CONCLUSION

Over the last two decades, as hope ensued that the peace dividend would create lasting peace and stability in Europe, the United States and NATO drew down their forces and significantly reduced their force posture in Europe. At the same time, NATO and the EU expanded, adding former Warsaw Pact states and former Soviet republics. In the last decade, Russia has increased its capability, and boldly employed them to pursue its objectives of increasing its influence in Europe, stopping the expansion of NATO and the EU, and creating fractures within Europe that enable Russia to exert influence on its own terms. This evolution has made it clear that based on current capabilities within the Alliance and the United States—particularly those forces stationed in Europe—the Alliance is not capable of preventing a Russian conventional attack into Alliance territory. This diminishes the Alliance's ability to deter Russia from using conventional or ambiguous threats to achieve its objectives to fracture the Alliance and gain influence in Europe. However, this does not preclude the possibility of enhancing conventional capabilities and developing other capabilities to counter ambiguous threats, which will in turn underpin a credible deterrence against Russian aggression. The way forward is to apply both types of deterrence—by denial and by punishment as described above—in order to provide a capable a credible deterrence both in the immediate and long-term. The consolidated effect of such efforts—to include forward presence, rotational forces, and combined and joint exercises and training—should increase the perceived costs and the probability of such costs in response to Russian aggression, and decrease the probability of Russia deriving benefits from its actions. The combined effect is a decrease in the value of the object for Russia, and an increase in the deterrent effect.

To develop such capabilities requires a concerted effort on the part of the United States, the Alliance, and the EU. It includes European NATO members continuing to search for more effective ways to increase capabilities and progressively increase their defense budgets. It also includes EUCOM and USAREUR to more effectively align their security cooperation activities to support capability development and a coordinated whole of government effort to address those capabilities that fall beyond the scope of the military, such as law enforcement. It is through such activities that the Alliance can develop a capable force that underpins the credibility of its commitment to defend Alliance territory through deterrence. The subsequent chapters of this monograph further elaborate on various aspects of U.S. Army efforts, in coordination with NATO and interagency partners, to achieve a credible and capable deterrent.

ENDNOTES - CHAPTER 2

1. Jim Garamone, "Dempsey Discusses Use of Military Instrument of Power," DoD News, U.S. Department of Defense website, July 2, 2014, available from *www.defense.gov/News-Article-View/Article/602812*, accessed December 5, 2015.

2. GEN Philip M. Breedlove, "Department of Defense Press Briefing by General Breedlove in the Pentagon Briefing Room," news transcript of a Pentagon briefing, Washington, DC, October 30, 2015, *www.defense.gov/News/News-Transcripts/Transcript-View/Article/626787/department-of-defense-press-briefing-by-general-breedlove-in-the-pentagon-brief*, accessed November 27,. 2015.

3. *Idem.,* "United States European Command Posture Statement 2016," Posture Statement presented to the 114th Congress,

2nd Session on February 25, 2016, Stuttgart, Germany: United States European Command, 2016, available from *www.eucom. mil/media-library/article/35164/u-s-european-command-posture-state ment-2016*, accessed February 27, 2016.

4. Carl von Clausewitz, *On War*, Michael Howard and Peter Paret eds./trans., Princeton, NJ: Princeton University Press, 1976, p. 92.

5. Gordon A. Craig and Alexander L. George, *Force and Statecraft: Diplomatic Problems of our Time*, New York: Oxford University Press, 1995, pp. 180-181.

6. Stephen L. Quackenbush, "Deterrence Theory: Where Do We Stand?" *Review of International Studies*, Vol. 37, No. 2, April 2011, p. 741, available from *search.proquest.com/docreview/87350 0712/fulltextPDF?accountid=4444*, accessed September 29, 2015.

7. Honorable Ashton Carter, "Strategic and Operational Innovation at a Time of Transition and Turbulence," Public speech at the Reagan National Defense Forum, Simi Valley, CA, November 7, 2015, available from *www.defense.gov/News/Speeches/Speech-View/Article/628146/remarks-on-s*, accessed on November 23, 2015. He stated: "We're modernizing our nuclear arsenal, so America's nuclear deterrent continues to be effective, safe, and secure, to deter nuclear attacks and reassure our allies."

8. The emergence of Islamic State in Iraq and Syria (ISIS) as a non-state actor with conventional capabilities presents a new twist on deterrence—that is, how to deter a non-state actor that could potentially pose a conventional threat to the United States. It is, however, not considered in the context of this monograph.

9. Thomas C. Schelling, *Arms and Influence*, New Haven, CT: Yale University Press, 1966, pp. 2-3.

10. Daniel Byman and Matthew Waxman, *The Dynamics of Coercion: American Foreign Policy and the Limits of Military Might*, New York: Cambridge University Press, 2002, pp. 1, 6.

11. John J. Mearsheimer, *Conventional Deterrence*, Ithaca, NY: Cornell University Press, 1983, p. 14.

12. Craig and George, p. 180.

13. Austin Long, *Deterrence From the Cold War to the Long War: Lessons from Six Decades of RAND Research*, Santa Monica, CA: RAND, 2008, p. 10.

14. Robert A. Pape, *Bombing To Win: Air Power and Coercion in War*, Ithaca, New York: Cornell University Press, 1996, p. 13.

15. Long, p. 10.

16. *Ibid.*, p. 35.

17. *Ibid.*, pp. 35, 74, and 93.

18. Craig and George, p. 180.

19. Byman and Waxman, pp. 10-12.

20. Craig and George, p.190.

21. *Ibid.*, p. 181.

22. Mearsheimer, p. 14.

23. Byman and Waxman, pp. 10-12.

24. Pape, pp. 1-54. While Pape's model focuses on coercion, he notes it equally applies to deterrence since the only difference between coercion and deterrence is that the former seeks to force the adversary to change its behavior, while the latter seeks to prevent him from changing his behavior. Based on the applicability of Pape's theories to coercion and deterrence, this monograph refers to Pape's approach using solely its application to deterrence (*Ibid.*, p. 4.).

25. *Ibid.*, pp. 15-16.

26. *Ibid.*, p. 16.

27. For example, as one snapshot in time, in 1989 at the tail end of the Cold War along the inter-German border (IGB), North

Atlantic Treaty Organization (NATO) forces consisted of more than 20 Allied divisions. (Refer to David A. Shlapak and Michael W. Johnson, *Reinforcing Deterrence on NATO's Eastern Flank: Wargaming the Defense of the Baltics*, Santa Monica, CA: RAND, 2016, p. 3, available from *www.rand.org/content/dam/rand/pubs/research_reports/RR1200/RR1253/RAND_RR1253.pdf, accessed* February 3, 2016.) Including tactical and strategic nuclear weapons that underpinned Cold War deterrence, and the second offset strategy employing precision guided munitions and the evolution of the air-land battle, one easily concludes the United States and NATO posed a credible and capable deterrence force against an equally large Soviet force. Applying Pape's logic of coercion, the costs would have been very high for the Soviet Union and the benefits minimal by going to war with NATO. The value of its objective would have likely been negative.

28. "Jane's Sentinel Security Assessment - Russia And The CIS," December 18, 2015, *https://janes.ihs.com/Janes/Display/1767799*, accessed April 28, 2016.

29. Shlapak and Johnson, p. 4,

30. Doug Mastriano *et al., Project 1704: A United States Army War College Analysis of Russian Strategy in Eastern Europe, and Appropriate U.S. Response and the Implications for U.S. Landpower*, Carlisle Barracks, PA: United States Army War College, 2015, p. 9.

31. Research discussions conducted from November 3-6, 2015, with the United States Mission to NATO, the United States Military Delegation to NATO, the NATO International Staff, Supreme Headquarters Allied Powers Europe (SHAPE), U.S. Army Europe (USAREUR), and U.S. European Command (EUCOM).

32. Honorable Robert Work, Deputy Secretary of Defense, "Deputy Secretary of Defense Speech—Royal United Services Institute (RUSI)," Whitehall, London, UK: Royal United Services Institute, September 10, 2015, available from *www.defense.gov/News/Speeches/Speech-View/Article/617128/royal-united-services-institute-rusi*, accessed October 28, 2015.

33. Elbridge Colby and Jonathan Solomon, "Facing Russia: Conventional Defence and Deterrence in Europe," *Survival*, Vol.

56, Iss. 6, November 2015, p. 21, *www-tandfonline-com.usawc.idm.oclc.org/doi/abs/10.1080/00396338.2015.1116146,* accessed November 30, 2015.

34. Robert D. Kaplan, "Countering Putin's Grand Strategy," *Wall Street Journal,* February 12, 2015, *search.proquest.com.usawc.idm.oclc.org/docview/1654552152,* accessed January 14, 2016.

35. There is a clear east-west divide: eastern NATO members perceive Russia as a significant threat, and the western NATO members do not. Other factors are creating divides as well, including the recent refugee crisis and the euro crisis. This refugee crisis is creating a potential north-south divide within the Alliance.

36. Rob Pritchard, "West accuses Russia of cyber-warfare," *Janes Intelligence Review,* December 29, 2014, available from *https://janes.ihs.com/Janes/Display/1732353,* accessed April 25, 2016.

37. Heather A. Conley, "Putin's Europe," in Craig Cohan and Melissa G. Dalton eds., *2016 Global Forecast,* Washington, DC: Center for Strategic and International Studies, 2015, p. 39, available from *csis.org/files/publication/151116_Cohen_GlobalForecast2016_Web.pdf,* accessed November 28, 2015.

38. Craig and George, p. 180.

39. President Barack Obama, "Remarks by President Obama to the People of Estonia," public speech, Nordea Concert Hall, Tallinn, Estonia, September 3, 2014, available from *https://www.whitehouse.gov/the-press-office/2014/09/03/remarks-president-obama-people-estonia,* accessed November 27, 2015.

40. Honorable Ashton Carter.

41. The White House, Office of the Press Secretary, "FACT SHEET: European Reassurance Initiative and Other United States Efforts in Support of NATO Allies and Partners," June 3, 2014, available from *https://www.whitehouse.gov/the-press-office/2014/06/03/fact-sheet-european-reassurance-initiative-and-other-us-efforts-support-,* accessed November 27, 2015.

42. Operation Atlantic Resolve is a demonstration of continued United States commitment to the collective security of NATO and to enduring peace and stability in the region, in light of Russia's illegal actions in Ukraine. From the United States Army Europe Atlantic Resolve web page, available from *www.eur.army.mil/atlanticresolve/*, accessed January 15, 2016. Additionally, U.S. European Command, Communication and Engagement Directorate, Media Operations Division, "OPERATION ATLANTIC RESOLVE (SEPTEMBER 2015)," United States European Command Fact Sheet on Operation Atlantic Resolve, September 2015, available from *www.defense.gov/Portals/1/features/2014/0514_atlanticresolve/docs/Operation_Atlantic_Resolve_Fact_Sheet_22SEP2015.pdf*, accessed 30 November 2015.

43. The NATO website states:

Due to the changed security environment on NATO's borders, the RAP includes 'assurance measures' for NATO member countries in Central and Eastern Europe to reassure their populations, reinforce their defence and deter potential aggression. Assurance measures comprise a series of land, sea and air activities in, on and around the NATO's eastern flank, which are reinforced by exercises focused on collective defence and crisis management. The RAP also includes 'adaptation measures' which are longer-term changes to NATO's forces and command structure so that the Alliance will be better able to react swiftly and decisively to sudden crises. Adaptation measures include tripling the strength of the NATO Response Force (NRF), creating a Very High Readiness Joint Task Force (VJTF) that is able to deploy at very short notice, and enhancing the Standing Naval Forces. To facilitate readiness and the rapid deployment of forces, the first six NATO Force Integration Units (NFIUs) - which are small headquarters - were inaugurated in Central and Eastern Europe. Headquarters for the Multinational Corps Northeast in Szczecin, Poland and the Multinational Division Southeast in Bucharest, Romania will be established along with a standing joint logistics support group headquarters.

North Atlantic Treaty Organization, "Readiness Action Plan," available from *www.nato.int/cps/en/natohq/topics_119353.htm*, accessed January 16, 2016.

44. North Atlantic Treaty Organization, "The NATO Defence (sic) Planning Process," available from *www.nato.int/cps/en/nato-live/topics_49202.htm*, accessed December 19, 2015. Through the NATO Defence (sic) Planning Process (NDPP), NATO identifies capabilities and promotes their development and acquisition by allies so that it can meet its security and defense objectives. By participating voluntarily in the NDPP, allies can harmonize their national defense plans with those of NATO. The NDPP is designed to influence national defense planning efforts and prioritizes NATO's future capability requirements, apportions those requirements to each ally as **targets**, facilitates their implementation and regularly assesses progress. NATO defense planning encompasses different domains; force, resource, armaments, logistics, C3 (consultation, command and control), civil emergency, air and missile defense, air traffic management, standardization, intelligence, military medical support, science and technology, and cyber.

45. One potential flaw of the NATO Defense Planning Process, particularly in light of the evolving security environment, is that capability targets are based on those capabilities that the Alliance needs in order to achieve its Level of Ambition (LOA). The LOA defines how many major and minor joint operations the Alliance should be able to simultaneously execute. Capabilities are not based on a threat, which has the potential risk of creating capability gaps, particularly as the threat continues to evolve at an ever-rapid pace.

46. North Atlantic Council, *Active Engagement, Modern Defence: Strategic Concept for the Defence and Security of the Members of the North Atlantic Treaty Organization*, Brussels, Belgium: NATO Public Diplomacy Division, November 2010, p. 30, available from *www.nato.int/strategic-concept/pdf/Strat_Concept_web_en.pdf*, accessed December 19, 2015.

47. Research discussions conducted on November 3, 2015, with the United States Mission to NATO, the United States Military Delegation to NATO, and the NATO International Staff.

48. Jan Techau, *The Politics of 2 Percent: NATO and the Security Vacuum in Europe*, Washington, DC: Carnegie Endowment for International Peace, Publications Department, September 2015, p. 4.

49. Luis Simón, "NATO's Rebirth: Assessing NATO's Eastern European 'Flank'," *Parameters,* Autumn 2014, p. 73.

50. Techau, p. 4.

51. Jens Stoltenberg, "Secretary General's Annual Report shows cuts in defence spending have almost stopped," NATO Press Release, January 28, 2016, available from *www.nato.int/cps/ en/natohq/news_127503.htm*, accessed February 27, 2016.

52. "Russia's Defence Budget," Jane's Defence Procurement Budgets, October 5, 2015, available from *https://janes.ihs.com/Janes/ Display/1327508#DEFENCE BUDGET TRENDS*, accessed January 14, 2016. Note: Caution should be taken in considering the amount of Russia's defense spending increase within the context of a corrupt society where not all defense spending actually goes toward defense investment.

53. The Security Insiders include: Gordon Adams, Charles Allen, Michael Allen, Thad Allen, Graham Allison, James Bamford, David Barno, Milt Bearden, Peter Bergen, Samuel "Sandy" Berger, David Berteau, Stephen Biddle, Nancy Birdsall, Marion Blakey, Kit Bond, Stuart Bowen, Paula Broadwell, Mike Breen, Mark Brunner, Steven Bucci, Nicholas Burns, Dan Byman, James Jay Carafano, Phillip Carter, Wendy Chamberlin, Michael Chertoff, Frank Cilluffo, James Clad, Richard Clarke, Steve Clemons, Joseph Collins, William Courtney, Lorne Craner, Roger Cressey, Gregory Dahlberg, Robert Danin, Richard Danzig, Janine Davidson, Daniel Drezner, Mackenzie Eaglen, Paul Eaton, Andrew Exum, William Fallon, Eric Farnsworth, Jacques Gansler, Stephen Ganyard, Daniel Goure, Mark Green, Mike Green, Mark Gunzinger, Todd Harrison, John Hamre, Jim Harper, Marty Hauser, Michael Hayden, Michael Herson, Pete Hoekstra, Bruce Hoffman, Linda Hudson, Paul Hughes, Colin Kahl, Donald Kerrick, Rachel Kleinfeld, Lawrence Korb, David Kramer, Andrew Krepinevich, Charlie Kupchan, W. Patrick Lang, Cedric Leighton, Michael Leiter, James Lindsay, Justin Logan, Trent Lott, Peter Mansoor, Ronald Marks, Brian McCaffrey, Steven Metz, Franklin Miller, Michael Morell, Philip Mudd, John Nagl, Shuja Nawaz, Kevin Nealer, Michael Oates, Thomas Pickering, Paul Pillar, Larry Prior, Stephen Rademaker, Marc Raimondi, Celina Realuyo, Bruce Riedel, Barry Rhoads, Marc Rotenberg, Frank Ruggiero, Gary Samo-

re, Kori Schake, Mark Schneider, John Scofield, Tammy Schultz, Stephen Sestanovich, Sarah Sewall, Matthew Sherman, Jennifer Sims, Suzanne Spaulding, James Stavridis, Constanze Stelzenmüller, Ted Stroup, Guy Swan, Frances Townsend, Mick Trainor, Richard Wilhelm, Tamara Wittes, Dov Zakheim, and Juan Zarate.

54. Sara Sorcher, "Security Insiders: NATO Unprepared to Counter Newly Aggressive Russia," *National Journal Daily A.M.*, April 28, 2014, available from *search.proquest.com/docview/1520022795*, accessed October 6, 2015.

55. The National Commission on the Future of the Army was established by the National Defense Authorization Act for Fiscal Year 2015 (Pub. L. 113-291). The Commission submitted a report containing a comprehensive study and recommendations to the President and Congress of the United States. The Commission examined the structure of the Army and policy assumptions related to the size and force mixture of the Army in order to make an assessment of the size and force structure of the Army's active and reserve components. The Commission made recommendations on modifications to the structure of the Army based on current and anticipated mission requirements, acceptable levels of national risk, in a manner consistent with available resources, and anticipated future resources. In accordance with legislation, the Commission specifically examined the transfer of Army National Guard AH-64 Apache attack helicopters from the Army National Guard to the Regular Army. The Commission consisted of eight Commissioners; four appointed by Congress and four appointed by the President. The Commissioners used their decades of public service and expertise in national and international security policy and strategy, military forces capability, force structure, organization, and employment, and reserve forces policy to provide recommendations that seek to strengthen the future Army. See National Commission on the Future of the Army website, Background, available from *www.ncfa.ncr.gov/content/background*, accessed April 28, 2016.

56. They used a Combat Power Builder and Combat Calculator (CBCC) model:

CBCC is an easy to use "first order" method to compare force design and actions at brigade or division levels in experimental, classroom, or field settings. The CBCC uses open source data to compute platform combat values, then, groups them into units. Opposing units are placed in 2-4 sectors where environmental and operational factors modify combat values to produce force ratios. The CBCC computes and displays losses in action (Offense or Defense) for 5-7 days, letting the user visualize the battle and draw or refine conclusions for more study.[5] Back-up Slides in the RSG briefing contain charts with supporting CBCC data.

See Douglas Macgregor, "MEMORANDUM FOR: National Commission on the Future of the Army (NCFA)," September 7, 2015, National Commission of the Future of the Army website, available from   *www.ncfa.ncr.gov/sites/default/files/COL%20%28R%29%20Douglas%20Macgregor--September%203%2C%202015.pdf*, accessed November 27, 2015, p. 2. They ran two scenarios using two different force constructs based on the current brigade combat team (BCT) structure, one using a single Stryker BCT and two Armored BCTs, and another with one Stryker BCT and two Armored BCTs. In both scenarios, the Russians defeated the United States forces nearly 80 percent of the time.

57. Shlapak and Johnson, pp. 4-6. RAND used a map-based tabletop exercise (TTX) in a series of war games. (*Ibid.*, p. 12). RAND further concluded that at least, in order to prevent a fait accompli, the United States would need to provide six or seven brigades, to include three heavy brigades, with enablers (*Ibid.*, p. 8).

58. John R. Deni, "NATO Force Posture upon Its Return to Europe: Too Little, Too Late," in Rebecca R. Moore and Damon Coletta, eds., *NATO's Return to Europe: Engaging Ukraine, Russia, and Beyond,* Washington, DC: Georgetown University Press, forthcoming in early 2017.

59. Charles F. Hermann, "Defining National Security," in John F. Reichart, Steven R. Sturm, eds., *American Defense Policy,* Baltimore, MD: Johns Hopkins University Press, 1982, available from *www.voxprof.com/cfh/hermann-pubs/Hermann-Defining%20National%20Security.pdf*, accessed October 22, 2015.

60. Office of the Under Secretary of Defense (Comptroller) Chief Financial Officer, *Defense Budget Overview: United States*

Department of Defense Fiscal Year 2017 Budget Request, Washington DC: Department of Defense, February 2016, table 7-7, available from *comptroller.defense.gov/Portals/45/Documents/defbudget/fy2017/ FY2017_Budget_Request_Overview_Book.pdf,* accessed February 27, 2016.

61. Staff Report, "Germany will deploy rotating infantry troops to Estonia in 2016," *The Baltic Times,* May 19, 2015, available from *www.baltictimes.com/germany_will_deploy_rotating_infan try_troops_to_estonia_in_2016/,* accessed February 27, 2016. Note: The reason Germany is critical is due to its influence in Europe, to include NATO and the European Union, and its close economic ties with Russia. Germany's participation would send a clear message to Russia that any armed aggression into Alliance territory would not be tolerated.

62. Under Article 3 of the North Atlantic Treaty, members are obligated to do all in their power to resist armed attack. It states:

> In order more effectively to achieve the objectives of this Treaty, the Parties, separately and jointly, by means of continuous and effective self-help and mutual aid, will maintain and develop their individual and collective capacity to resist armed attack.

North Atlantic Treaty Organization, "The North Atlantic Treaty," April 4, 1949, available from *www.nato.int/cps/en/natolive/official_ texts_17120.htm,* accessed February 3, 2016.

63. Research discussions conducted between November 5-6, 2015, with USAREUR, and EUCOM.

64. United States Joint Chiefs of Staff, *Joint Operation Planning,* Joint Publication 5-0, Washington, DC: United States Joint Chiefs of Staff, August 11, 2011, pp. III-3 – III-42, available from *www. dtic.mil/doctrine/new_pubs/jp5_0.pdf,* accessed November 28, 2015.

65. Research discussions conducted between November 5-6, 2015, with USAREUR and EUCOM staff, and with various staff elements in the Pentagon on October 27, 2015.

66. The author concluded, following 3 years at EUCOM as a political-military affairs desk officer, that the Department of Defense does a poor job of preparing staff officers for such jobs (refer to R. Reed Anderson, "Political-Military Affairs Officers - The Art of Strategic Planning," *FAO Journal*, Vol. XII, No. 4, October 2009, pp. 14-20, available from *www.faoa.org/resources/Documents/pub40.pdf*, accessed November 28, 2015). Based on discussions conducted between November 5-6, 2015 with USAREUR and EUCOM staff, this appears still to be the case and the Department of Defense should look at ways of resolving this professional development shortfall.

67. According to NATO's website:

> CFI is a key enabler in developing the goal of NATO Forces 2020: a coherent set of deployable, interoperable and sustainable forces equipped, trained, exercised, commanded and able to operate together and with partners in any environment. It is essential in ensuring that the Alliance remains well prepared to undertake the full range of its missions, as well as to address future challenges wherever they may arise. In light of the current security environment, it is also a means to deliver the training and exercise elements of the Alliance's Readiness Action Plan.

"Connected Forces Initiative," NATO website topics, available from *www.nato.int/cps/en/natolive/topics_98527.htm*, accessed January 16, 2016.

68. Deanne Corbett, "Germany To Buy Back Tanks Amid Russia Threat," *Defense News,* April 18, 2015, available from *www.defensenews.com/story/defense/land/vehicles/2015/04/18/germany-to-buy-back-tanks-amid-russia-threat/25879281/*, accessed January 14, 2016.

69. Franklin D. Kramer *et al., NATO's New Strategy: Stability Generation*, Washington, DC: The Atlantic Council, 2015, p. 1, available from *www.atlanticcouncil.org/publications/reports/nato-s-new-strategy-stability-generation*, accessed April 14, 2016.

70. Joseph F. Pilat, "Reassessing Security Assurances in a Unipolar World," *The Washington Quarterly*, Vol. 28, No. 2, Spring 2005, p. 159.

71. *Ibid.*, p. 159.

72. See, for example, Jeffrey W. Knopf, ed., *Security Assurances and Nuclear Nonproliferation,* Stanford, CA: Stanford University Press, 2012.

73. The White House, Office of the Press Secretary.

74. See for example, "Cavalry ride: American forces in Europe" *The Economist (Online),* Apr 1, 2015, available from *search. proquest.com.usawc.idm.oclc.org/docview/1669491275,* accessed November 30, 2015.

75. As defined by its Level of Ambition (LoA) which defines the number, scale, and nature of the military operations that NATO should be able to conduct simultaneously, North Atlantic Council, *NATO Handbook,* Brussels, Belgium: NATO Public Diplomacy Division, 2006, p. 53, available from *www.nato.int/docu/ handbook/2006/hb-en-2006.pdf,* accessed December 19, 2015.

76. Kramer *et al.*

77. Agence France-Presse, "Russia Expands Military Exercises To 80,000 Troops," March 15, 2015, available from *www. defensenews.com/story/defense/international/europe/2015/03/ 19/russia-expands-military-exercises-troops/25023979/,* accessed 30 November 2015.

78. Arnold Wolfers, "National Security as an Ambiguous Symbol," *Political Science Quarterly,* Vol. 67, No. 4, December 1952, pp. 481-493, available from *www.jstor.org.usawc.idm.oclc.org/ stable/2145138?pq-origsite=summon&seq=1#page_scan_tab_contents,* accessed October 24, 2015.

CHAPTER 3

THE TIME-DISTANCE CHALLENGE
OF U.S.-BASED FORCES

> Presence is important, because presence equals trust.
> You can't rotate trust. You can't surge trust. You earn
> trust in long-term relationships. Our ability to use
> these European bases to project on behalf of the alli-
> ance or other objectives is about that trust, that rela-
> tionship, that long-term bond you get from forward-
> stationed forces.
>   —General Philip Breedlove[1]

Events similar to the one in this monograph's opening vignettes are becoming more and more familiar in
Eastern Europe as tensions increase between Russia
and North Atlantic Treaty Organization (NATO).[2] The
European Leadership Network highlighted 40 events
in just 8 months in 2014, stating that:

> these events add up to a highly disturbing picture of vio-
> lations of national airspace, emergency scrambles, nar-
> rowly avoided mid-air collisions, close encounters at sea,
> simulated attack runs and other dangerous actions hap-
> pening on a regular basis over a very wide geographical
> area.[3]

On March 5, 2014, in a statement before the Senate Armed Services Committee, U.S. Secretary of Defense Chuck Hagel announced that the Department
of Defense (DoD) was boosting its NATO presence
by taking additional steps to reassure its Baltic allies
in the face of Russia's aggressive actions in Crimea.[4]
This effort included increased U.S. Air Force contributions to NATO's Baltic Air Policing mission and
increased U.S. Army contributions to ground exer-

cises in Estonia, Latvia, Lithuania, and Poland.[5] These new missions would eventually become Operation ATLANTIC RESOLVE[6] and by October 2015, U.S. Army Europe (USAREUR) soldiers had participated in multinational events from the Baltic States to the Black Sea.[7] Lithuania's land forces commander Major General Almantas Leika stated the movement of U.S. Army forces into the region "shows that we can rely on our ally."[8]

In 2015 the Commander of U.S. Air Forces Europe (USAFE), General Frank Gorenc stated:

> When [the crisis in] Crimea broke out, from the word go to the time that the F-15 showed [up] in Lithuania was 14 hours. You can't replicate that without forward-based combat power. I still get thank-you's from the Baltic countries with respect to that. They were completely assured and very, very happy that we did that.[9]

This deployment was considered a major strategic success and the blistering 14-hour response time highlighted a unique capability of the air domain. However, these missions were flown during peacetime (between NATO and Russia) and in a permissive environment. If the Russian Army advanced into Baltic territory, it would operate under a layered protective umbrella of advanced Russian surface-to-air missile systems. Additionally, Russia has 27 combat Air Force squadrons in its Western Military District alone.[10] In war game scenarios, NATO airpower appears unable to generate enough sorties to stop Russia from taking two of the three Baltic capitals in 60 hours.[11] Furthermore, any forward-based airpower would be subject to continuous SS-26 Iskandar missile attacks which, combined with the surface-to-air missile threat, would force NATO airpower to fly missions from Scandinavia or Western Europe.[12] Russia has essentially created an Anti-Access Area Denial (A2/AD) region for NATO airpower and seapower in the Baltic region. Although Russia's A2/AD systems appear dormant in peacetime, that could change at the flip of a switch. As the USAREUR Commander Lieutenant General Ben Hodges stated:

> Readiness to perform any mission is why we are forward stationed in Europe. Though we make up only 5% of the Army's manpower, US Army Europe touches or is involved in most of what the US Army delivers in terms of strategic effect...we guarantee access to allies and critical infrastructure. US Army Europe enables early entry so we don't have to do forced entry.[13]

Despite the benefits of forward-based military power, both USAFE and USAREUR have endured similar infrastructure and force structure reductions (over 70 percent in the last 25 years).[14] USAREUR in particular consists of only about 30,000 soldiers and maintains only two assigned maneuver forces: the 173d Airborne Infantry Brigade Combat Team (IBCT) and the 2nd Cavalry Regiment (2CR). There is no armor or attack aviation assigned to USAREUR.[15] To mitigate a plausible Russian attack, USAREUR relies on the Army's Regionally Aligned Forces (RAF) concept to better prepare for potential contingencies.[16]

This chapter argues that continental United States (CONUS)-based Regionally Aligned Forces do not provide the Army a reliable, enduring mechanism to overcome the time/distance challenge inherent in a Baltic conflict with Russia. To overcome the time/distance challenge that Russia could exploit, the DoD should assign, allocate, and apportion forces versus aligning them, to include assigning a two-star head-quarters (HQ) to USAREUR, and establishing a rotational allocation of an Armored Brigade Combat Team (ABCT) that provides a continuous rotational presence of armor in Europe.

THE PROBLEM OF A RESURGENT RUSSIA

The previous chapter noted RAND's findings that based on current capabilities of the forces stationed in Europe, the United States, and NATO lack the capability to defeat Russian aggression should Russia, using both conventional and ambiguous warfare, choose to invade the Baltic States. However, this does not preclude NATO from developing such capabilities and associated activities (forward presence, rotational forces, combined/joint exercises, and training) that will in turn underpin a more credible deterrent to Russian aggression. Improving NATO capabilities, activities, and forward-presence force posture are likely to change the cost/benefit analysis for Russia to increase deterrence. To be effective, a deterring force must be credible, capable, and have the will to fight. Traditionally, no force fits that description better than the U.S. military. However, in the last 20 years USA-REUR alone has decreased from about 300,000 soldiers to 30,000.[17] In addition to this drawdown in American forces (prior to the Russian invasion of Ukraine and the subsequent Wales Summit), overall defense spending of NATO members dropped.[18]

As discussed in Chapter 1, Russia's key foreign policy goals are the protection of its homeland through the creation and maintenance of an external buffer zone and the protection of the Russian diaspora that live in the so-called near abroad. Russia has proven that it is willing to use military force against neighbors to further these policy goals. Like Ukraine, the three Baltic States were republics that gained independence after the fall of the Soviet Union and have large Russian minorities.[19] While no one can predict whether, when, or where Russia might again violate another state's sovereignty, the United States would be wise to better posture its military forces to support other NATO members against potential Russian aggression. General Hodges recognizes that with a much smaller forward-based force structure than it had during the Cold War, USAREUR has to look to other methods to reassure allies and respond to possible Russian aggression.[20] One method that the Army has developed is the RAF concept.

REGIONALLY ALIGNED FORCES

General Ray Odierno introduced the RAF concept in 2013 to compensate for a strategy to resources mismatch saying "nothing is as important to your long term success as understanding the prevailing culture and values."[21] General Odierno defined the RAF as:

> Army units and leaders – Brigades, Divisions, Corps, and support forces – who focus on a specific region within their normal training program by receiving cultural training and language familiarization.[22]

USAREUR's current aligned forces are the 4th Infantry Division (4ID) as USAREUR's RAF division HQ and the 1st Brigade, 3rd Infantry Division (1/3ID) as the RAF ABCT. Regional alignment is an:

> organizing policy that improves the Army's ability to provide responsive, specifically trained, and culturally attuned forces to support Combatant Command (CCMD) requirements.[23]

The RAF includes active duty, Army National Guard, and Army Reserve personnel of all force pool categories (Assigned, Allocated, and Service Retained-CCMD Aligned [SRCA]).[24] RAF units essentially fulfill requirements outside of the global force management process to assist Geographic Combatant Commanders (GCC) in fulfilling Theater Campaign Plans (TCP). RAF forces can also conduct shaping operations like those assigned forces typically conduct. This allows the Army to keep more SRCA forces in reserve for contingencies. Aligned forces regionally train to the readiness level required by the CCMD to which they are aligned.[25] Additionally, baseline training will be supplemented by regional skills appropriate for their anticipated missions.

The term "aligned" is not a joint term used in global force management. According to the Center for Army Lessons Learned, "despite their regional mission and training focus, SRCA forces can be allocated by the Secretary of Defense in accordance with global force management business rules to meet a higher priority requirement."[26] In other words, regionally aligned forces are still open to traditional sourcing options anywhere in the world regardless of the region to which the Army aligned the forces and regardless of the mission for which the forces have trained. This has the potential to waste money, time, and effort. For example, 4ID is only aligned to USAREUR for 2 years. Because 4ID is not assigned or allocated to USAREUR, it is open to other possible mission assignments. Moreover, there is no indication that 4ID will continue to be aligned to USAREUR after its initial commitment. This is not the expectation of partners and allies in the field, where many assume that 4ID would be available to USAREUR or U.S. European Command (EUCOM) in the event of crisis.[27]

Source: Staff Sgt. Caleb Barrieau, *www.army.mil/media/370520.*

General Raymond Odierno, then Army Chief of Staff, talks with multinational soldiers participating in exercise Combined Resolve III at the Hohenfels Training Area, Germany, November 4, 2014. The exercise featured the U.S. Army's regionally aligned force for Europe, at the time the 1st Brigade Combat Team, 1st Cavalry Division, which supported the EUCOM during Operation ATLANTIC RESOLVE. The current Regionally Aligned Force consists of the 4th Infantry Division and the 4th Infantry Division Mission Command Element and the 1st Armored Brigade Combat Team, 3rd Infantry Division. The shifting of units assigned the RAF mission is not conducive to long-term relationships with local partners and allies.

Figure 3-1. Regionally Alligned Forces.

This is not conducive to long-term relationships with local partners and allies, such as those that General Breedlove spoke of in the epigraph. To reduce confusion and uncertainty as well as to synchronize Army concepts with joint partners, EUCOM should work with the Joint Staff to have such Army forces assigned, allocated or apportioned to EUCOM rather than just relying on the Army to align them. Such guidance should be codified in the Global Force Management Implementation Guidance (GFMIG), and specific allocation of forces identified in the Global Force Management Allocation Plan (GFMAP). Providing clear guidance and identification of forces not only allows units to properly prepare for potential and assigned missions, but also provides EUCOM continuity in force planning in support of shaping operations and contingency planning.

TYPES OF FORCES

Joint Publication (JP) 5-0, *Joint Operation Planning*, describes only three processes to manage U.S. forces: assignment, allocation, and apportionment.[28] Assigned forces belong to a CCMD and are used to perform missions assigned to that command. Allocated forces are either assigned or unassigned (service retained) forces that are then transferred by the Secretary of Defense (with the President's approval) to a new commander, generally from one CCMD to another. Allocation comes in two forms; emergent and rotational and while allocation issues are handled by the Global Force Management Board (GFMB), the Secretary of Defense decides the final allocation.[29] Although emergent allocation happens quicker than rotational allocation, it still must go through the Pentagon bureaucracy and requires the Joint Staff to modify the GFMAP.[30] Apportionment is the distribution of forces for planning purposes only.[31]

According to a recent RAND report, Russia maintains approximately 22 maneuver battalions in its Western Military District and Kaliningrad Oblast with arguably many more battalions available if it shifts emphasis from Ukraine.[32] Through extensive wargaming, RAND demonstrated that Russian forces would be able to seize two of the three Baltic capitals (Tallinn and Riga) in approximately 36-60 hours and assessed the outcome as a "disaster for NATO."[33] RAND concluded, "NATO's current posture is inadequate to defend the Baltic [S]tates from a plausible Russian conventional attack."[34] Of note, the force posture RAND analyzed included the 82nd Airborne Division's Global Response Force (GRF) that is postured to send one battalion-sized element within 18 hours.[35] This worst-case surprise attack could present NATO with the conquest and occupation of NATO's Baltic members as a fait accompli and suggests that neither emergent allocation nor regional alignment is responsive enough to protect the three Baltic States. For more effective deterrence, (or for a more plausible posture to prevent Russian conquest) NATO forces will need to be in the area, ready to fight when hostilities begin.[36] From a U.S. perspective, the forces needed would most likely be USAREUR's two assigned brigades and any rotational unit that was in place by coincidence at the time. However, continuously rotating allocated units would mitigate the lack of response time by, and potential unavailability of, the U.S. Army's aligned forces. Rotational allocation allows the force provider time and flexibility to identify and prepare units, in advance, for an operation.[37]

Although apportioned forces may not be the ones actually used during execution of an operation, they aid deliberate planning. Generally, apportioned forces are tied to an operations plan (OPLAN) and provide planners with notional forces to assist the development of planning assumptions and guidance. Now that the Pentagon is reportedly updating contingency plans for an armed conflict with Russia, the Secretary of Defense should apportion Army forces to EUCOM to aid the development of a future OPLAN.[38] Regardless of how forces are assigned, allocated, or apportioned, USAREUR needs to be able to build and maintain regional expertise without losing flexibility.

AN ASSIGNED HEADQUARTERS

The U.S. Army War College's Project 1704 offered four courses of action to counter the Russian approach to the Baltic States that covered a wide array of diplomatic, information, military and economic (DIME) actions. One consistent theme across all options was the need for a two-star HQ.[39] Not only does an assigned HQ demonstrate American resolve, it "would foster the relationships, trust, expertise, and oversight required to integrate U.S. rotational forces with other NATO and host nation capabilities."[40] According to Stephen Covington, undermining Europe's political cohesion is a key target for Russian President Putin.[41] Covington assesses that Russia benefits from a distracted Alliance focused on challenges outside the Russian sphere of influence.[42] In a presentation to the School of Advanced Military Studies, General Hodges said:

> We have non-stop exercises going on from Estonia to Bulgaria — the [ATLANTIC RESOLVE] series of exercises. We are doing more than 50 exercises this year alone that are battalion or larger. We are also doing exercises in Ukraine, Georgia and back in Germany. So, you can imagine with our small number of units, in order to spread that effect, we have captains in several countries that are the senior United States commander in that nation.[43]

While giving young U.S. Army officers and non-commissioned officers an opportunity to lead is beneficial, USAREUR is forced to direct an orchestra without a conductor.[44] In an address to the U.S. Army War College, Deputy Secretary of Defense Bob Work described a single infantry battalion deployed to Afghanistan that had been disaggregated into 77 different units.[45] The Deputy Secretary recognized that small units spread out over wide areas have huge implications for leadership, especially in today's net-centric environment.[46] In a reference to RAF HQ, General Hodges noted:

> I would be completely unable to do what we're doing now if we did not have the 4th Division headquarters…they are essential to us being able to provide the assurance and deterrence that we're doing.[47]

USAREUR's mission statement is to train and lead Army Forces in support of EUCOM by:

- Training and preparing full spectrum capable forces for global employment;
- Strengthening alliances and building partner capacity and capability;
- Providing Army Service Component Command and Title 10 support; and,[48]
- Continually seeking to improve the readiness and quality of life of Soldiers, Army Families and Civilian workforce.[49]

Despite the U.S. military's can-do attitude, USAREUR does not have the capacity to effectively handle the day-to-day business of Operation ATLANTIC RESOLVE in addition to its normal organize, train, and equip (OT&E) mission. HQs are the often underappreciated brains of an operation. Typically, assigned forces, National Guard State Partnership Program (SPP) and the Army Reserve's military-to-military training program forces are the units that conduct the peacetime shaping operations that assure allies and deter potential adversaries. However, this mission is now falling on regionally aligned and rotational forces that do not maintain an enduring presence. These units cannot be expected to capture lessons learned above the tactical level nor establish and maintain key long-term relationships among allies and interagency partners. This critical component of shaping the environment is best accomplished by a two-star Joint Task Force-capable HQ.[50] In dealing with Russia, USAREUR should seek a strategy that balances ends, ways, and means. A two-star HQ is the right size to achieve that balance, enabling U.S. forces to more effectively plug into any number of corps-level HQs across Europe, including NATO's Multinational Corps Northeast based in Poland.

In order to train for this sort of multinational engagement, NATO created six new command, control, and reception entities called NATO Force Integration Units (NFIU). These units have been active since September 2015 and are expected to reach full operational capability in 2016.[51] They are located throughout Eastern Europe (Bulgaria, Estonia, Latvia, Lithuania, Poland, and Romania) to work:

> in conjunction with host nations to identify logistical networks, transportation nodes and supporting infrastructure to ensure NATO high-readiness forces can deploy into an assigned region as quickly as possible.[52]

NFIUs would work in close coordination with the Allied Joint Force Command Brunssum (JFC Brunssum) through NATO's Allied Land Command in Izmir, Turkey. It is unclear whether the RAF or other rotational forces would integrate into this command and control structure through the USAREUR staff, or whether it would accomplish this through a small rotational Mission Command Element (MCE). With respect to HQs, Conrad Crane suggests that the way to provide stability on the ground is through an established HQ however, "we are often playing the Super Bowl with a pickup team."[53] When crises arise, there are many times when there is a scramble to fill the void, often with ad hoc, untrained personnel. Crane warns, "the complexity of contemporary warfare requires well-trained and coordinated staffs capable of providing detailed planning and comprehensive intelligence at every level. That aspect of warfighting must be enhanced, not cut."[54]

All of these efforts would be even more complicated if EUCOM were to publish an OPLAN in Europe. Secretary of Defense Ashton Carter alluded to this in a recent speech saying, "we are adapting our operational posture and contingency plans as we — on our own and with allies — work to deter Russia's aggression."[55] It is likely that such a plan would initially be classified and would require some level of coordination with host nation personnel as well as foreign militaries. A recent RAND assessment of overseas basing concluded that a sizable reduction in HQ units would affect strategic and operational level engagement.[56] To preserve the HQ capability and keep command structures intact, forces should be returned when operational needs merit or if OPLANS determined certain forces need to be in place.[57] Russia's recent activity and the subsequent response by the United States suggest that operational needs merit a return of an assigned HQ.

Currently the 4ID at Fort Carson is controlling Operation ATLANTIC RESOLVE efforts in Europe using a 90-man MCE. General Hodges commented on the MCE:

> Fourth division command post arrived just the other day. The deputy commander has touched every one of the embassies and the defense leadership of all the nations of Operation [ATLANTIC RESOLVE (OAR)], and he and the fourth Division Mission Command element are going to be running land operations for OAR all year. So getting that level of headquarters is really a huge help to us.[58]

However, it is inefficient to have an HQ develop such relations temporarily only to have another HQ have to go through the same thing later. Obviously, this is better than nothing, but a command post and an MCE will not provide the capacity and strategic messaging of an assigned two-star HQ nor the continuity of assigned forces. Further, a standing two-star command would be able to establish standard operating procedures for coordination and integration with the NFIUs. Finally, if Russia made a surprise move into the Baltic region, an MCE could not be expected to perform as a joint forces land component HQ capable of coordinating joint land operations and activities, to include joint reception, staging, onward movement, and integration (JRSOI) for the joint force, and potentially allied land forces in support of land operations.

Source: U.S. Army Photo by Sgt. James Avery, 16th Mobile Public Affairs Detachment, *www.army.mil/media/400896*.

Lithuanian Land Forces Colonel Dalius Polekauskas, Chief of Staff, Lithuanian Land Forces, (left) shakes hands with U.S. Brigadier General Michael J. Tarsa, deputy commanding general for support, 4th Infantry Division out of Fort Carson, CO, after he and the 4th ID's Mission Command Element arrived at Vilnius International Airport, Vilnius, Lithuania, July 1, 2015. This monograph argues that a two-star, Joint Task Force-capable headquarters is needed in Europe.

Figure 3-2. Mission Command Element.

Qualitative efforts matter to Russia and U.S. allies. Current Army efforts are ad hoc and quantitative in nature. However, in the Spring of 2015, Russia conducted an extensive command and control exercise for a multi-theater conventional war stretching from the Baltic States to the Arctic.[59] Russia has changed the security environment in the Baltic States and has set a "course to compete over Europe's future security arrangement."[60] Although Russia may not want a war with the West, an assigned division HQ in Europe is an appropriate enduring move to reassure allies, focus shaping and deterrence operations, and to fight a war if needed. Small, rotational HQs with ad hoc formations cannot deliver the depth of engagements that a permanently assigned, appropriately staffed HQ can.

PROVIDING THE COMMANDER FLEXIBLE OPTIONS: A CASE FOR ARMOR

Equipment not in the region at the start of hostilities will face a significant challenge getting there in time to affect the outcome. The current balance of power in northeastern Europe favors Russia, not NATO. The Alliance will need heavy forces able to quickly respond in the unlikely, albeit feasible, case of a Russian *coup de main*.[61] If not, under that scenario, Russian forces could be in Riga, Latvia; and Tallinn, Estonia in no less than 60 hours, leaving NATO with only bad options.[62]

Another complicating factor is that the United States and NATO lack sufficient indication and warning capabilities to forecast Russian moves. General Breedlove told the Senate Armed Services Committee in April 2015 that Ukraine underscored critical gaps in collection and that Russian military exercises were a continued surprise.[63] General Hodges remarked to Defense News, "I've been watching the Russian exercises . . . what I cared about is they can get 30,000 people and 1,000 tanks in a place really fast. Damn, that was impressive."[64] In one exercise, just before Christmas 2014, the Russians massed 250 tanks and armored personnel carriers on the Lithuanian border inside the Kaliningrad Oblast.[65]

NATO's response has been the RAP, promulgated at the 2014 Wale's Summit. The plan involved "enhancing the NATO Response Force (NRF) to make it more responsive and capable."[66] Essentially, it would grow from 13,000 to 40,000 troops. Additionally, it created a new lead unit called the Very High Readiness Joint Task Force (VJTF) comprised of a multinational brigade of around 5,000 soldiers supported by air, maritime, and Special Forces.[67] With the help of NFIUs, the VJTF may be able to move within the hoped-for timeline of less than 7 days.[68] However, activating these new forces would require the consensus of the North Atlantic Council (NAC) as well as national approval, and could move too slow to counter further Russian aggression.[69] Therefore, a more realistic timeline is closer to 10 days, and even perhaps as many as 28 days. Moreover, the VJTF and NRF remain outnumbered by the Russian units in the Western Military District and Kaliningrad Oblast, and would be susceptible to advanced Russian A2/AD capabilities if, due to late NAC approval, the units arrived after the commencement of hostilities.[70]

In 2005, the Overseas Basing Commission was concerned about resident landpower in Europe, specifically armor, recommending that a heavy brigade combat team (BCT) should remain in Europe, fully manned, and that another heavy BCT equipment set should be prepositioned in the region.[71] Despite the warning, both of USAREUR's heavy BCTs were deactivated, removing much of USAREUR's armored force and more than 10,000 soldiers.[72] Moreover, the United States was not the only Alliance member that reduced its armored forces in Europe. Twenty years ago, Germany fielded three armored corps consisting of 2,200 tanks, but today it has only 250.[73] All of Russia's forces in the Baltic region, including its eight airborne battalions, are motorized, mechanized, or tank units.[74] Just 2 years after removing armor from Europe, the United States is scrambling to return some capability to the region by spreading over 200 tanks and Bradley fighting vehicles around Estonia, Latvia, Lithuania, Poland, Romania, and Bulgaria as part of the European Activity Set (EAS) in support of rotational deployments.[75] Commenting on the armor's arrival, General Hodges stated, "of course, our allies, they see tanks, they see Bradleys, they see self-propelled howitzers. That significantly increases the sense of assurance, which is the primary reason for doing it."[76]

Unfortunately, the presence has not been continuous. Armored units are only scheduled to be present in Europe for 9 of the next 18 months—that is, only 50 percent of the time. Some suggest the lack of continuous presence of a rotational armor force is born out of the fear of provoking Russia (versus deterring it).[77] Russia has overwhelming numerical superiority over NATO forces in the Baltic region. U.S. strategic communications efforts should highlight that a returning ABCT provides senior leaders with flexibility and assures allies. The final chapter will further explore this vital element of the information environment as a way to mitigate risk.

In Donbass, eastern Ukraine, Russia effectively used ambiguous warfare tactics to paralyze decision-making.[78] If Moscow employed similar tactics, vis-à-vis NATO, and was able to slow down Alliance decision-making, NATO's response might be too slow to thwart Russian aggression. Russia also used its modern, layered air defense system to keep Ukrainian close air support aircraft and attack aviation out of the fight.[79] Further, Russian tanks were well protected by reactive armor and central to land operations in the region.[80] According to a Center for Naval Analyses (CNA) review of the fighting Russia used armored raids deep into Ukrainian territory.[81] Russian artillery accounted for 85 percent of Ukrainian casualties and light infantry fighting vehicles simply could not survive.[82] The bottom line from the CNA report is that "mounted infantry need tank-equivalent protection."[83] Russia learned much from its fight in Georgia where Georgian T-72 tanks had better navigation, imaging, and communication than Russian T-72s. Essentially this left Russian tanks blind at night and in poor weather, which Russia has since fixed by upgrading its tanks.[84] The counter to this is resident landpower. If the Alliance had three ABCTs in the Baltic region at the time of Russian aggression, NATO could delay the fait accompli by at least 7 days, the time it would take for the VJTF to arrive.[85]

If the United States is drawn into combat in the Baltic region (most likely in conjunction with invocation of a NATO Article 5-based response) it will not be like Iraq or Afghanistan. The fighting in eastern Ukraine is state-sponsored warfare on a high-tech, high-intensity battlefield where Russian armed forces have superiority (or at least parity) in many domains.[86] In a recent speech in Estonia, President Obama promised to uphold America's Article 5 treaty obligations to the three Baltic States. The President's words set clear ends but the current ways and means to back up that policy with military force are not particularly credible in preventing Russian conquest. It is unclear how the United States and the rest of the Alliance could accomplish their collective defense objectives after a fait accompli by Moscow.

A key step in that defense is to return an ABCT to Europe, with a primary focus on rotations in the Baltic States and Eastern Europe, in a continuous rotational presence. While ambiguous warfare is getting all of the attention and understandably, much discussion revolves around how to counter it, Russia's last few wars have demonstrated its willingness and ability to fight conventionally with a reliance on landpower as its primary means of warfare.[87] Moreover, combining an ABCT with the resident capabilities of the 2CR and 173d Airborne IBCT will provide commanders with a better menu of options to include mil-to-mil training with other partner armored-units and shaping operations. The decision by the United States to withdraw armor from Europe was based on the idea that Russia was a positive contributor to the security situation in Europe—it has proven that is no longer the case. A fully manned and equipped ABCT should be rotationally allocated to Europe until the strategic calculus changes again.[88]

Although Secretary of Defense Carter recently announced that a portion of the fiscal year 2017 budget will "go toward putting a 'heel-to-toe' ABCT in Europe,"[89] the budget is for 2017, still needs to be approved by Congress and implemented by the Department of the Army. Despite this new budget request announcement that occurred at the time of this writing, the recommendation remains valid. Additionally, as a new administration arrives in office, it will decide how to best handle decisions laid on it by previous leadership. One continuous ABCT is the right balance—any more force structure could provoke Russia and exhaust U.S. Army means, yet any less would leave the Baltic States unacceptably exposed.

Source: U.S. Army photo by Spc. Marcus Floyd, 13th Public Affairs Detachment, *https://www.flickr.com/photos/usarmyeurope_images*.

Soldiers participating in Saber Strike 15 conduct a combined live fire exercise June 19, 2015 at the Drawsko Pomorskie Training Area in Poland. A heel-to-toe rotation of armor units in Europe is needed.

Figure 3-3. A U.S. Armor Presence in Europe.

MULTILATERALIZING THE SOLUTION SET: A CASE FOR AN ALLIED APPROACH

There are several steps NATO should consider in order to maximize its ability to deter Russia while individual allies such as the United States modify force structure in Europe. First, NATO should re-examine its Supreme Allied Commander Europe's (SACEUR) authority to reposition forces in Europe. Currently, SACEUR cannot move forces without a North Atlantic Council Execution Directive. There are several reasons for resistance among the allies to grant this approval. One reason is that the allies are reluctant to grant what would amount to permission to put their forces in harm's way without approval from their capitals and discussions at NATO HQ. Another reason is that funding is a national responsibility. Costs lie where they fall and very little comes out of the commonly funded pool of resources. The bulk of NATO's €3 billion common funding is spent on the International Security Assistance Force (ISAF) mission, communications, and the Airborne Warning and Control System (AWACS) platform. If SACEUR could reposition forces under his own authority, he would essentially have the ability to commit funds of the ally from which the forces originated.

Many members of the Alliance have national governments that are very leery or constitutionally prohibited from allowing anyone to commit national funding. For this reason, NATO should re-examine how it funds contingency operations. SACEUR needs the authority to reposition forces at the first indications of a Russian threat and if national funding is the prohibitive factor, NATO needs to update its funding mechanisms. SACEUR would also have the ability to employ these authorities as a part of the theater security cooperation-enabled NATO exercise program.

Source: NATO photo by British Army Sergeant Ian Houlding, *https://www.flickr.com/photos/usarmyeurope_images.*

Drawsko Pomorskie Training Area, Poland—The NATO flag is raised during the opening ceremony for Exercise Steadfast Jazz November 2013 at the Drawkso Pomorskie Triaining Area in Poland. NATO plays a critical role that the United States can help facilitate, but should not carry the load for the Alliance.

Figure 3-4. NATO's Role.

Second, NATO should move toward a multinational logistics capability. Collective defense for small countries in Europe is a critical piece of their budget calculations. In general, it makes more financial sense to specialize in a few areas, while allowing others to specialize in other areas. The main concern remains that the other countries will need to provide the capability when it is required. This was less of a challenge for U.S. forces based in Europe during the Cold War, since the United States maintained all the capabilities it needed on the continent. Four Divisions and two Corps HQs in the Cold War era construct provided not only the war fighting capability, but the combat service support (CSS) and combat support (CS) capability that U.S. formations would require in the event of a conventional conflict with the Soviet Union. In the modern era, U.S. forces forward-based in Europe have decreased and the CSS and CS units that supported the corps and divisions (and their subordinate units) have largely disappeared. As a result, the United States will need to rely heavily on support to arrive from CONUS or on capabilities that are already on the continent.

When NATO was initially conceived, logistics was a national responsibility. In the new construct, it will not be possible for the United States to support conventional combat operations with national assets. In fact, in several recent computer war games, the logistics tail is what brought the United States to a halt in the fighting—national assets could simply not get enough fuel and ammunition forward fast enough to allow the U.S. formations to continue to attack.[90] In order to go to a NATO universal logistics capability, it would have to be commonly funded. Of the top four contributors to NATO funding (Germany, United Kingdom, France, and the United States), the United Kingdom and France appear unsupportive of developing a common logistics system because they would continue to bear a disproportionate share of the funding burden.

Third, NATO should streamline the timeline for approvals of counter-Russia actions. While many acknowledge the need to be faster to meet realistic timelines to counter or deter Russian action, current staff processes are insufficient to allow for this action. NATO needs to come to an agreement on a common assessment and a counter-Russia plan (Baltic-focused). Then the Alliance must designate the force that would execute the mission, before it is needed. With these three areas agreed upon ahead of time, the VJTF may be able to meet a 10-day employment timeline, consistent with the 7-day deployment timeline envisioned for the VJTF.[91] These pre-completed steps along with increased authority for SACEUR could greatly reduce the employment timelines for forces. When these timelines are rehearsed as part of the NATO exercise program, they will reinforce the Alliance's ability to assure member states and will show Russia a credible and capable deterrent force.

Finally, NATO should reinitiate dialogue with Russia. As recently as 10 years ago, there were conversations in NATO about the Russians joining the Alliance. In light of Russian action in Crimea and Ukraine, these conversations have stopped. As NATO moves toward re-establishing a deterrent capability and conducting increased exercises in what may be contentious areas, increased transparency will become critical to ensuring there are no misunderstandings or accidental escalations.

CONCLUSION

Two NATO capitals are potentially 60 hours from being in Russian control.[92] Chapter 2 argued that the United States and NATO must be capable of deterring Russian land forces; Russian special operations forces (SOF), particularly when used in an ambiguous role; and Russian information operations (IO), which will be discussed in Chapter 5. Small, displaced units operating alone in the three Baltic States may not be the best way to convey a focused, capable, credible commitment to Russia.

The recommendations in this chapter are intended to reassure allies by strengthening capabilities that will, in turn, enhance credible conventional deterrence of potential Russian aggression in the Baltic region. Specifically, the DoD should assign, allocate, and apportion forces versus aligning them, and EUCOM should push to have a two-star HQ assigned to USAREUR, and an apportioned continuous rotational presence of an ABCT in Europe.

An assigned two-star HQ is key to focusing a broad range of efforts, working with allied and interagency partners, countering enduring Russian IO, capturing lessons learned, and preparing rotational forces. The HQ would be the culturally savvy caretakers of key relationships. Allocated and apportioned units would then be free to focus on readiness until they entered a well-set theater. Asking units to do more (outside of a surge) in today's operational tempo is unrealistic. Army Chief of Staff General Mark Milley issued a memorandum to the Army that stated, "readiness for combat is our No.1 priority and there is no other No. 1."[93]

The United States cannot afford to reassure allies to the point where they rely entirely on the United States to ensure their security. HQ staff is the appropriate level to maintain visibility on this sensitive and complex issue. After all, the Alliance is the center of gravity, it seems imprudent to rely on a small MCE or reach back to an HQ 4,000 miles away.

The United States should increase the amount of available armored forces in Europe by instituting continuous presence of one U.S. ABCT. The 2005 Overseas Basing Commission recommended leaving American armor in Europe to reassure and train allies and to deter potential adversaries. Russia, on the other hand, has upgraded its armor and effectively used it in its wars with Georgia and Ukraine. This leaves the 2CR, the 173d Airborne IBCT, and 11 Baltic infantry battalions exposed to a numerically superior armor force.[94] Although NATO has made some headway since the Wales Summit in developing the VJTF, rotationally allocated armor in Europe is the appropriate move to give NATO time to show up. Admittedly, the challenge in Europe is not just a U.S. Army one—instead it is a challenge facing all of NATO.

Indeed the alliance could play an important role in helping to mitigate the time-distance challenge presented by the lack of a massive U.S. military presence on the continent. The United States must focus less on how to "make 30,000 look like 300,000"[95] and more on how to leverage the over 300,000 NATO soldiers who are already in Europe. When there were 300,000 U.S. troops with the necessary support capability, it was certainly easier to accomplish critical tasks. If the NATO process was slow or unwieldy, SACEUR could put on his EUCOM hat and authorities to accelerate the process. The problem in Europe today is that there are only so many U.S. forces available to execute tasks under those authorities. Until force posture changes, the "NATO solution" will remain a critically important element of the broader solution set.

ENDNOTES - CHAPTER 3

1. John Vandiver, "Breedlove: No-fly zone over Syria would constitute 'act of war'," May 21, 2013, *Stars and Stripes*, available from *www.stripes.com/news/breedlove-no-fly-zone-over-syria-would-constitute-act-of-war-1.223788*, accessed December 1, 2015.

2. Thomas Frear, Lukasz, and Ian Kearns, "Dangerous Brinkmanship: Close Military Encounters Between Russia and the West in 2014," Policy Brief, November 2014, European Leadership Network, available from *www.europeanleadershipnetwork.org/medialibr ary/2014/11/09/6375e3da/Dangerous%20Brinkmanship.pdf*, accessed April 26, 2016.

3. *Ibid.*

4. "Pentagon sending fighter jets to boost NATO presence amid Ukraine crisis 2014," *Fox News*, March 5, 2014, available from *www.foxnews.com/politics/2014/03/05/hagel-says-us-stepping-up-support-to-nato-allies-in-europe-amid-ukraine-crisis/*, accessed August 26, 2015.

5. Association of the United States Army, "The U.S. Army in Europe: Strategic Landpower in Action," Torchbearer Campaign Issue Paper, October 2015, p. 4.

6. *Ibid.*, p. 2.

7. *Ibid.*

8. *Ibid.*

9. Aaron Mehta, "Interview: USAF Gen. Frank Gorenc," *Defense News*, March 10, 2015, available from *www.defensenews.com/story/defense/2015/03/10/interview-usaf-gen-frank-gorenc/24701435/*, accessed December 1, 2015.

10. David A. Shlapak and Michael W. Johnson, *Reinforcing Deterrence on NATO's Eastern Flank: Wargaming the Defense of the Baltics*, Santa Monica, CA: RAND, 2016, p. 3, available from *www. rand.org/content/dam/rand/pubs/research_reports/RR1200/RR1253/ RAND_RR1253.pdf*, accessed February 3, 2016.

11. *Ibid.*

12. Kaarel Kaas, "Russian Armed Forces in the Baltic Sea Region," *Diplomaatia*, No. 130/131, June/July 2014, available from *www.diplomaatia.ee/en/article/russian-armed-forces-in-the-baltic-sea-region/*, accessed February 15, 2016.

13. Lieutenant General Ben Hodges, "Remarks by Lt. Gen. Ben Hodges, Commanding General, U.S. Army Europe (USAREUR)," Speech at the USAREUR Change of Command ceremony, Wiesbaden, Germany, November 5, 2014.

14. Association of the United States Army, p. 2.

15. United States Army Europe official website, Units and Commands, available from *www.eur.army.mil/organization/units.htm*, accessed February 21, 2016.

16. Tom Roeder, "General: Army plans to rely more heavily on Fort Carson soldiers to counter Russian aggression," *The Gazette*, September 20, 2015, available from *gazette.com/general-army-plans-to-rely-more-heavily-on-fort-carson-soldiers-to-counter-russian-aggression/article/1559637*, accessed March 2, 2016.

17. John R. Deni, *The Future of American Landpower: Does Forward Presence Still Matter? The Case of the Army in Europe*, Carlisle, PA: Strategic Studies Institute, U.S. Army War College, 2012, p. 2.

18. *Ibid.*

19. Shlapak and Johnson, p. 3.

20. David Vergun, "USAREUR commander: Eastern Europe troop rotations likely to continue," November 24, 2014, available from *www.army.mil/article/138877/USAREUR_commander__Eastern_Europe_troop_rotations_likely_to_continue/*, accessed March 2, 2016.

21. General Ray Odierno, "Regionally Aligned Forces: A New Model for Building Partnerships," March 22, 2012, available from *armylive.dodlive.mil/index.php/2012/03/aligned-forces/*, accessed February 21, 2016.

22. *Ibid.*

23. Army Capabilities Integration Center website, Regionally Aligned Forces (RAF), available from *www.arcic.army.mil/Initiatives/regionally-aligned-forces.aspx*, accessed December 1, 2015.

24. *Ibid.,* note: Service Retained- Combatant Command (CCMD)-Aligned (SRCA) is not a joint doctrinal term. The Army uses it to define a pool of forces from which it draws forces to support the RAF. The three joint doctrine terms for Global Force Management include: assigned, allocated, and apportioned, which this monograph goes on to further explain.

25. Kimberly Field, James Learmont, and Jason Charland, "Regionally Aligned Forces: Business Not As Usual," *Parameters,* Vol. 43, No. 3, Autumn 2013, p. 60.

26. Center for Army Lessons Learned, *Regionally Aligned Forces Brigade Planning,* Handbook 16-06, Fort Leavenworth, KS: Center for Army Lessons Learned, November 2015, p. 77.

27. Throughout the research process, the team encountered confusion over the RAF at all levels of the Army, the joint team, and NATO. Multiple discussions at U.S. European Command (EUCOM) and USAREUR suggests that there is a reasonable expectation that the RAF are the forces that will be brought forward during a contingency. While most understand the Global Force Management (GFM) process, there is belief that RAF are being "held" for the regions they are aligned to. Further discussions at US Army G-3 suggest this is not the case.

28. U.S. Joint Chiefs of Staff, *Joint Operation Planning,* Joint Publication 5-0, Washington, DC: United States Joint Chiefs of Staff, August 11, 2011, p. H-1.

29. *Ibid.,* p. H-2.

30. *Ibid.*

31. *Ibid.,* p. H-1.

32. Shlapak and Johnson, p. 4.

33. *Ibid.*

34. *Ibid.*

35. Drew Brooks, "Global Response Force Acts as a 911 for the U.S. March 11, 2015, available from *www.emergencymgmt.com/safety/Global-Response-Force-911-for-US.html*, accessed February 21, 2016.

36. Shlapak and Johnson, p. 1.

37. U.S. Joint Chiefs of Staff, p. H-3.

38. Julie Ioffe, "Exclusive: The Pentagon Is Preparing New War Plans for a Baltic Battle Against Russia" *Foreign Policy*, September 18, 2015, available from *foreignpolicy.com.usawc.idm.oclc.org/2015/09/18/exclusive-the-pentagon-is-preparing-new-war-plans-for-a-baltic-battle-against-russia/*, accessed January 3, 2016.

39. Doug Mastriano *et al.*, *Project 1704: A United States Army War College Analysis of Russian Strategy in Eastern Europe, and Appropriate U.S. Response and the Implications for U.S. Landpower*, Carlisle Barracks, PA: United States Army War College, 2015, p. 100.

40. *Ibid.*

41. S.R. Covington, *Putin's Choice for Russia*, Cambridge, MA: Harvard Kennedy School Belfer Center for Science and International Affairs, 2015, pp. 12-13.

42. *Ibid.*

43. Stephen P. Kretsinger Sr, "Hodges discusses Army challenges in Europe," September 24, 2015, available from *www.ftleavenworthlamp.com/article/20150924/NEWS/150929733*, accessed February 21, 2016.

44. Quote developed during author's interview with Dr. Richard A. Lacquement Jr., Dean, United States Army War College School of Strategic Landpower, Carlisle Barracks, PA, December 22, 2015.

45. Deputy Secretary of Defense Bob Work, "Army War College Strategy Conference," Speech at the U.S. Army War College, Carlisle Barracks, PA, April 8, 2015.

46. *Ibid.*

47. Michelle Tan, "Army looks to rotating and reserve forces for Europe missions," *Army Times,* October 8, 2015, available from *www.armytimes.com/story/defense/show-daily/ausa/2015/10/08/army-looks-rotating-and-reserve-forces-europe-missions/73289458/,* accessed October 30, 2015.

48. In other words—organizing, training, and equipping U.S. Army Forces for EUCOM.

49. United States Army Europe official website, Mission Statement, available from *www.eur.army.mil/organization/mission.htm,* accessed April 26, 2016.

50. This headquarters (HQ) should be an operational theater Joint Task Force (JTF) capable of coordinating TSC activities, ongoing operations, joint reception, staging, onward movement, and integration (JRSOI) for all services and Allied land forces in support of NATO operations. This HQ should also be capable of commanding unilateral U.S. operations until such time that the NATO command structure assumes command and control.

51. NATO Supreme Headquarters Allied Powers Europe (SHAPE) website, "NATO Force Integration Units," September 2015, available from *https://www.shape.nato.int/operations/nato-force-integration-units,* accessed February 21, 2016.

52. NATO (SHAPE) website, "NATO Response Force / Very High Readiness Joint Task Force," Fact Sheet, Supreme Headquarters Allied Powers Europe, available from *aco.nato.int/page349011837,* accessed October 30, 2015.

53. Conrad Crane, "Observations on the Long War," September 10, 2014, War on the Rocks website, available from *warontherocks.com/2014/09/observations-on-the-long-war/,* accessed December 30, 2015.

54. *Ibid.*

55. Eric Zuesse, "U.S. Secretary of Defense Ashton Carter Implies Russia and China Are 'Enemies' of America. What Next?" *Global Research*, November 11, 2015, available from *www.globalresearch.ca/u-s-secretary-of-defense-ashton-carter-implies-russia-and-china-are-enemies-of-america-what-next/5487984*, accessed November 30, 2015.

56. Michael J. Lostumbo *et al.*, *Overseas Basing of U.S. Military Forces: An Assessment of Relative Costs and Strategic Benefits*, Arlington, VA: RAND Corporation, 2013, pp. 292-294.

57. *Ibid.*

58. "Interview: Lt. Gen. Ben Hodges," *DefenseNews*, March 31, 2015, available from *www.defensenews.com/story/defense/policy-budget/leaders/interviews/2015/03/27/lt-gen-ben-hodges/70573420/*, accessed December 5, 2015.

59. Covington, p. 10.

60. Covington, p. 14.

61. Shlapak and Johnson, p. 1.

62. *Ibid.*

63. "Senate Armed Services Committee Opening Statement by General Phil Breedlove, Commander, U.S. European Command," April 30, 2015, available from *eucom.mil/media-library/article/33031/senate-armed-services-committee-opening-statement-by-general-phil-breedlovecommander-u-s-european*, accessed December 5, 2015.

64. "Interview: Lt. Gen. Ben Hodges," *DefenseNews*.

65. Damien Sharkov, "Putin Orders Snap Military Drills on NATO Border," *Newsweek*, December 16, 2014, available from *www.newsweek.com/putin-orders-snap-military-drills-russian-troops-nato-border-292308*, accessed December 5, 2015.

66. NATO website, "NATO's Readiness Action Plan," Fact Sheet, North Atlantic Treaty Organization, February

2015, available from *www.nato.int/nato_static_fl2014/assets/pdf/pdf_2015_02/20150205_1502-Factsheet-RAP-en.pdf*, accessed December 30, 2015.

67. *Ibid.*

68. NATO (SHAPE) website, "NATO Response Force / Very High Readiness Joint Task Force"

69. Interviews with international officers at SHAPE, November 3, 2015.

70. Interviews with international officers at SHAPE, November 3, 2015. Also, Shlapak and Johnson, p. 4.

71. Overseas Basing Commission, Al Cornella *et al.*, *Report of the Commission on Review of the Overseas Military Facility Structure of the United States*, Arlington, VA: United States Congress, May 2005, p. C&R4.

72. Dakota L. Wood ed., *2016 Index of U.S. Military Strength: Assessing America's Ability to Provide for the Common Defense*, Washington, DC: The Heritage Foundation, 2015, p. 86.

73. Shlapak and Johnson, p. 8.

74. Shlapak and Johnson, p. 5.

75. John Vandiver and Matt Millham, "Carter: US to Position Armor in Baltics, Poland, Southern Europe," June 23, 2015, available from *www.military.com/daily-news/2015/06/23/carter-us-to-position-armor-in-baltics-poland-southern-europe.html*, accessed December 5, 2015.

76. "Interview: Lt. Gen. Ben Hodges," *DefenseNews.*

77. Throughout interviews, the team encountered the opinion that returning armor to Europe may provoke Russia. While the team agrees that Russia will use the information domain to spin that message, the balance of power is heavily on Russia's side and that USAREUR could counter Russian propaganda with that message.

78. Mary Ellen Connell and Ryan Evans, "Russia's 'Ambiguous Warfare' and Implications for the U.S. Marine Corps," CNA's Occasional Paper, Arlington, VA: CNA Analysis and Solutions, May 2015, p. 10.

79. Connell and Evans, p. 12.

80. *Ibid.*

81. *Ibid.*

82. *Ibid.*

83. *Ibid.*

84. Mastriano *et al.*, p. 57.

85. Shlapak and Johnson, p. 1.

86. Connell and Evans, p. 19.

87. Mastriano *et al.*, p. 47.

88. Mastriano *et al.*, p. 131.

89. Jen Judson, "Army Budget Boosts European Presence Sacrifices Modernization," *Defense News*, February 6, 2016, available from *www.defensenews.com/story/defense/policy-budget/2016/02/05/army-budget-boosts-european-presence-sacrifices-modernization/79884226/*, accessed March 2, 2016.

90. Information derived from a review of a classified war game after action report conducted by the U.S. Army War College, Center for Strategic Leadership-Strategic Wargaming Division, December 15, 2015.

91. Information derived from research discussions with SHAPE staff members conducted by the author on November 4, 2015.

92. Shlapak and Johnson, p 1.

93. Amanda Dolasinski, "Army leaders: Combat readiness is No. 1 priority," *Fayetteville Observer*, October 14, 2015, available from *www.fayobserver.com/military/army-leaders-combat-readiness-is-no-priority/article_5e35ccb2-f3e5-59e2-a758-aeed7e68876b.html*, accessed March 2, 2016.

94. Shlapak and Johnson, p 4.

95. Benjamin Hodges, "Strong Europe" Lecture at the U.S. Army War College, Carlisle Barracks, PA, September 21, 2015.

CHAPTER 4

THEATER SECURITY COOPERATION IN EUROPE: KEY TO CONVENTIONAL DETERRENCE

> EUCOM will...participate in...bilateral and multilateral exercises and engagements to support the mission to assure and defend NATO, enhance Allied and partner ability to provide for their own security, and counter Russia's use of conventional, irregular, and asymmetric warfare.
> —General Philip Breedlove, U.S. European Command (EUCOM) Commander[1]

As a North Atlantic Treaty Organization (NATO) staff officer at Supreme Headquarters Allied Powers Europe (SHAPE) stated, "NATO is like car insurance. It is something you continually pay against for a distant, even remote, possibility. It can become very expensive in the long run—even if you never need it."[2] As the size of forces in Europe has decreased, the ability of NATO to present a credible and capable deterrent to Russian actions has also decreased. In order to present a credible deterrent to conventional Russian aggression, NATO members will need to become more integrated, agile, and comfortable relying on other members' capabilities. The United States with its decreased force structure in Europe can no longer bear the lion's share of the burden alone. As the allies move toward more integrated operations, General Philip Breedlove's excerpt from his theater strategy above will drive how this deterrent effect will be possible. The interaction he describes meets the U.S. definition for theater security cooperation (TSC),[3] which, as noted in the 2015 *Guidance for the Employment of the Force* (GEF), "is a way to achieve desired ends, not an end unto itself."[4] Focused, joint, and multinational TSC—including foreign internal defense—will remain a key pillar of a deterrent strategy for a Russian non-nuclear threat in Europe. TSC, done properly with the right focus can ensure that NATO presents a credible, capable, and ready force to counter Russian aggression.

The remainder of this chapter will focus on the most dangerous course of action; that of a conventional attack, as well as address ways to deter Russian use of ambiguous means, considered the most likely course of action. The efforts to address the most likely and most dangerous courses of action are presumed to address the most disruptive course of action as defined in Chapter 1.

ACHIEVING A DETERRENT EFFECT

A Russian incursion into the Baltic States may be unlikely, but if the threat of a conventional attack is possible under certain conditions, the question becomes how to deter the Russian threat adequately without becoming provocative or opening up a new security dilemma. As seen in war games, the Russians have the ability, with very little indications and warnings, to mass forces and seize the Baltic States. As noted in previous chapters, various analyses have shown that the lack of permanent U.S. and other NATO forces (other than those of the Baltic NATO members) and the geography of the region would enable Moscow to seize the Baltic States within 60 hours. No matter how the scenario is played, without a significant force already present in the Baltic States, NATO always loses (although this does not account for the deterring effect of force presence addressed in Chapters 2 and 3 of this monograph).[5] According to one NATO official:

> In the end, I have no doubt that NATO will prevail and that we will restore the territorial integrity of any NATO member [but] I cannot guarantee that it will be easy or without great risk.[6]

The amount of damage and instability such an assault and re-conquest would incur would be tremendous. In essence, the best way for NATO to win a conventional fight in the Baltic States (or Eastern Europe) is not to fight one.

Outnumbered and out-positioned, the challenge for NATO becomes how to deter Russia from taking conventional action. As seen earlier in this monograph, deterrence theory provides two methods of deterring an opponent from achieving its goals. Deterrence through threat of punishment postulates that the action one side is taking will not be worth the cost that will be exacted on it from the other side.[7] NATO armies, continental United States (CONUS)-based U.S. forces, the Global Response Force (GRF), and Regionally Aligned Forces (RAF) based in CONUS are valid tools for deterrence by punishment. Although their arrival would be delayed, and they would have to overcome Russian Anti-Access Area Denial (A2/AD) systems, the follow-on forces would most likely have the ability to forcibly eject Russian forces from the Baltic States. This deterrence by punishment will remain a key portion of any calculus Russian President Vladimir Putin uses before taking conventional action. However, as noted in Chapter 1, President Putin is an opportunist and if he saw a window to take the Baltic States in a fait accompli manner and then negotiate for favorable terms before NATO marshals a sufficient force for a counterattack, he might do so.

The other means of deterring an opponent is through denial. At its core, deterrence by denial is producing an environment, through either physical presence or capability that denies the adversary the ability to accomplish even short-term goals. At first glance, deterrence by denial seems an easy and obvious answer to the deterrent problem with respect to Russia. If NATO is able to posture forces in such a quantity and array that Russia is unable to accomplish even short-term goals, then the Alliance has won without fighting. What makes this a less practical solution is the problem of numbers. Lieutenant General Ben Hodges frequently mentions that his struggle is to "make 30,000 look like 300,000."[8] His statement is a reference to the Cold War force numbers for U.S. Army troops permanently based in Europe. The current numbers of 30,000 are nowhere near the levels of the height of the Cold War. The armed forces of the rest of the allies have shrunk as well.

While modern forces are much more effective than Cold War troops due to advances in technology, air support, and training, their numbers preclude them from being spread across Europe as they were in the 1970s and 1980s. The old General Defense Plans that had multiple NATO corps headquarters (HQs) and numerous NATO divisions are no longer viable; and it is impossible to deter by denial through sheer physical occupation of terrain.

The question quickly becomes, if conventional deterrence by punishment will be incredibly costly on both sides and deterrence by denial is not very practical, how should NATO exert its efforts? As discussed in Chapter 2, in order to deter behavior, the deterrence must be credible and capable. Credibility comes from the adversary actually believing that the opposing side has the will to take action. Capability comes from the adversary believing the opposing side has the means to take effective action should it choose to do so. NATO provided a credible and capable deterrent force during the Cold War, but currently this is an open question. The NATO Warsaw Summit in July 2016 will likely be a key turning point in the discussion of NATO's force posture on the continent. In the meantime, assuming the United States will maintain a Stryker Brigade Combat Team (SBCT) and an Airborne Infantry Brigade Combat Team (IBCT), that Congress will approve the President's request for a rotational Armored Brigade Combat Team (ABCT), and that current NATO force posture will remain generally the same, a key pillar to a deterrent strategy against conventional Russian aggression in Europe will remain TSC.

THEATER SECURITY COOPERATION: ENABLING DETERRENCE

The GEF defines security cooperation as follows:

Security Cooperation: Security cooperation encompasses all DoD interactions with foreign defense establishments to build defense relationships that promote specific US security interests, develop allied and friendly military capabilities for self-defense and multinational operations, and provide US forces with peacetime and contingency access to a host nation. It is a way to achieve desired ends, not an end unto itself.[9]

Unless the U.S. force posture in Europe significantly changes, TSC is the primary means by which the United States can contribute to NATO's improved conventional deterrence capability. As the definition indicates, TSC is a broad term for any interaction between the U.S. Department of Defense (DoD) and foreign security establishments. How the United States chooses to spend its time and money as it relates to NATO remains of critical importance. As a NATO staffer shared, internal to NATO, "budgets and force structure have shrunk away from building collective defense capacity to capacity-building focused on non-NATO forces."[10] This was a reference to not only the International Security Assistance Force (ISAF) mission in Afghanistan, but also to the focus among the Alliance more on partners in Europe and less on the collective defense mindset.

Currently, the United States employs three lines of effort underneath a TSC umbrella: the European Reassurance Initiative (ERI); country-specific Security Cooperation plans; and bilateral/multilateral NATO exercises. The GEF directs:

> In light of resource constraints, whenever possible, Country specific cooperation sections [for a Theater Campaign Plan] should support regional approaches … in order to achieve regional economies of scale.[11]

The GEF's direction is especially appropriate with respect to Europe. While TSC can focus on specific countries, it should also take a regional approach, gaining "regional economies of scale." The struggle for the United States TSC efforts is the balance between U.S. Embassy country team focus areas, U.S. European Command (EUCOM) focus areas, and NATO capability targets. While the three are not always mutually exclusive, they are frequently not mutually supporting either.

Source: 112th Mobile Public Affairs Detachment Photograph by First Lieutenant Paul Nadolski/Released, *www.eucom.mil/media-library.*

Dragoons from Iron Troop, 3rd Squadron, 2nd Cavalry Regiment, maneuver through a forest toward a simulated enemy stronghold. Their mission was to capture a high value target as part of a combined training exercise with Estonian Allies in support of Operation ATLANTIC RESOLVE, March 7, 2015, in Rabassare, Estonia. Theater security cooperation is a key pillar to enabling deterrence.

Figure 4-1. Theater Security Cooperation.

When ERI emerged in June of 2014, it was an attempt to quickly reassert the U.S. commitment to NATO and to Europe. The additional funding for operations and exercises allowed EUCOM to increase its activity across the theater, conducting highly visible training events that served to broadcast to European citizens the continued U.S. commitment to the Alliance.

At its introduction, ERI was very well received by European populations. At this point, however, the allies appear to understand the United States is committed to NATO, but they want to see concrete efforts to deter Russia. The United States is at a point now where the friendly focused reassurance effort needs to shift to NATO-based, Russian-focused deterrence.[12]

The second line of effort, country-specific TSC, is focused on a balance of what the U.S. Embassy country team and the relevant combatant command (CCMD), working together, have determined is important, on the capability targets that have been assigned by NATO HQ to Alliance members, and on what individual allies and partners are interested in and capable of absorbing. As military forces shrink in Europe, these capability targets have become increasingly valuable. In theory, national specialization, based on NATO assigned goals, ensures countries strive to bring their assigned capabilities to the Alliance. In practice, this is not always the case, and many nations rely on the United States as a safety net for their assigned tasks.

A U.S. Army Europe (USAREUR) staff member likened the current approach of country-specific TSC to exercising in a gymnasium. In his analogy, the United States was the spotter and the other NATO countries were all bench-pressing weights. At the first sign of struggle, the United States swoops in and immediately pulls the weight off the chest of the struggling ally. While this relief has the short-term impact of reassuring the ally that the United States will always be there in their time of need, it has the long-term impact of failing to allow the ally to develop the appropriate "muscle" and does not actually make them stronger — instead it creates an enduring attitude of dependence on the United States.[13]

The third component to ongoing TSC efforts is the numerous exercises and named operations occurring in Europe. Exercise Trident Juncture 15 (a NATO Very High Readiness Joint Task Force [VJTF] exercise including the U.S. GRF), Operation ATLANTIC RESOLVE (Baltic defense operation), and Exercise Fearless Guardian (Ukraine advise and assist mission) all allow NATO to focus its energy on specific areas. U.S. forces in Europe are incredibly busy. Units are quickly moving from one exercise to the next, simultaneously reassuring allies, training capabilities, and rehearsing for future contingency operations. As the United States looks to the future, it will need to apply appropriate thought and focus to its exercise program. It remains important to tie exercises to the required collective capabilities and to ensure NATO allies are integrated based on their capability targets as well as what NATO needs them to do for the Alliance. In an article in *Military Review*, two former Army Service Component Command staff members advocate for a holistic approach to TSC:

> A successful security planning process will curtail purposeless or episodic activities with limited potential for long-term impact [and answer] [w]hy are we doing this activity and how does it support our goals and objectives in theater?[14]

As the United States re-examines its goals for TSC and specifically for its exercise program, it must ensure that it answers the previous question, and the CCMD must nest all components of its TSC plan within the NATO exercise program. As the United States assists with shaping this program, the planners would be well served to remember the six theater priorities from the EUCOM theater strategy of October 2015 (listed in priority):

- Deter Russian Aggression;
- Enable the NATO Alliance;
- Preserve United States Strategic Partnerships;
- Counter Trans-national Threats;
- Ensure Postured and Ready Forces; and,
- Focus on Key Relationships.[15]

Source: U.S. Army photo by Sergeant Brandon Anderson, 13th Public Affairs Detachment/Released *https://www.flickr.com/photos/usarmyeu rope_images.*

Soldiers of Company D, 2nd Battalion, 7th Infantry Regiment, 1st Armored Brigade Combat Team, 3rd Infantry Division, and Danish soldiers of Dragoon Regiment, 1st Armored Battalion, 1st Danish Tank Squadron, participated in a combined arms live fire exercise at the Drawsko Pomorskie Training Area, Poland June 16, 2015 as part of Exercise Saber Strike 15. The exercise sought to facilitate cooperation amongst the United States, Estonia, Latvia, Lithuania, and Poland to improve joint operational capability in a range of missions as well as preparing the participating nations and units to support multinational contingency operations. There were more than 6,000 participants from 13 different nations. Conducting the right exercises at the right scale is a challenge that EUCOM and USAREUR should work together in coordination with NATO allies and partners.

Figure 4-2. Exercise Saber Strike 2015.

There are three ways that TSC can continue to support the six priorities. TSC can support the U.S. Embassy country team's requirements, accomplish EUCOM-TSC guidance, and serve as building block events that culminate into a major NATO exercise. While the first two are important, the maximum gain for the United States comes from the integration of TSC building blocks into a NATO exercise. In this case, the countries get the training they need and a high-end exercise has the added benefit of a deterrent effect toward Russian activity, especially in the Baltic States. Unfortunately, with the mechanics of budgeting within NATO, General Breedlove, in his Supreme Allied Commander Europe (SACEUR) role, has extremely limited ability to conduct "snap-exercises" to either test readiness or to position forces near a potential conflict site in order to deter. Moving national forces can incur financial cost for the owning ally and many countries within the Alliance are hesitant to allow the military leader of another ally the right to spend national funds. This concern, while understandable, places large limitations on NATO's ability to use exercises as a deterrent tool prior to the onset of actual hostilities.

EXERCISE-BASED DETERRENCE

In response to Russian ambiguous activities and its enhanced conventional military power, NATO and the United States need to re-examine their deterrent posture. In order for deterrence to be effective, it must be capable and credible, and that starts with a robust NATO exercise-based deterrent strategy. A NATO exercise-based deterrent strategy must demonstrate several distinct aspects in order to present a capable signature.

The NATO exercise program must be highly visible with well-publicized exercises that reflect how and where NATO would defend against a real Russian attack. Exercises should replicate as closely as possible the conduct of the operational plans and should be joint and multinational. The design of the exercises must clearly communicate their defensive nature and information operations (IO) should reinforce that it is a response to unwanted aggression on the part of Russia, a point further explored in Chapter 6.

As they rehearse pieces of the operational plan, the exercises should also rehearse "a visible approach for flowing reinforcements and materiel to forward forces quickly, securely, and assuredly."[16] Logistics shortfalls emerge in every iteration of a Baltic defense war game and therefore, NATO must show the Russians that it has the capability to ensure its forces can continue to fight for the long term. A theoretical example would involve a combined German battalion and Stryker Squadron moving by rail from Germany to Poland, disembarking in Poland, moving through Poland and the Suwalke Gap with NATO air support, linking up with Lithuanian forces, and conducting several days of defensive exercises. An additional enhancement would be the deployment of U.S. armored forces using pre-positioned equipment in Poland with a follow-on movement through the Suwalke Gap. NATO-controlled resupply operations would support the drill.

Although briefly described here, such an operation would be incredibly challenging to execute and would also have to be carefully messaged to the Russians to ensure that its defensive nature was understood. Russian observers would need to be invited to participate in the entire operation to ensure Moscow was aware of both the nature and the effectiveness of the operation.

USAREUR has begun to take steps in this direction with its participation in the Polish National Anakonda exercise scheduled for June 2016. From its beginnings as a Polish national training event, it has morphed into a large, multinational exercise that incorporates multiple types of forces and locations. Unfortunately, after the exercise began to take shape, elements within the NATO command structure declined to provide command and control for the event. The provided reason was that the exercise was too provocative toward the Russians from a NATO perspective.[17]

Source:*https://www.flickr.com/photos/usarmyeurope_images/24539 314710/in/album-72157661903283323/.*

Exercise Anakonda 16 is a Polish-led, joint, multinational exercise taking place in Poland from June 7-17, 2016. This exercise involves more than 25,000 participants from 21 nations. Anakonda 16 is a capstone event for USAREUR and partner nations which will set conditions for success at the NATO biannual summit in July 2016 in Warsaw, Poland. Anakonda 16 validates the requirements set at the NATO Wales Summit in September 2014 in time for members of the alliance to reconvene at the Warsaw summit in July.

Figure 4-3. Anakonda Rock Drill.

In order to maximize the credibility of NATO's enhanced deterrence posture, NATO must demonstrate that it is willing to rapidly approve and move forces from the various staging locations to an area of conflict on a timeline that would keep it competitive with a Russian timeline. The centralized nature of decision-making on the Russian side, which greatly streamlines the decision-making timeline, coupled with their ability to move forces discretely along interior lines, will make it a challenge for NATO to beat the deployment timeline, but it must do better.

In the past, NATO relied on having forces close to the locations where they would fight to streamline processes. Units would probably already have been in the fight before the approvals came out of Brussels. The situation has changed and forces are no longer staged near the locations where they would fight. NATO recognized that it would need a force that could quickly move in reaction to NATO's needs to reinforce its eastern border. The VJTF was built to fill this need. For reasons noted in Chapter 3, it is probably unrealistic for the VJTF (NATO's quickest response force) to make it to the Baltic States in less than 28 days, which is clearly an unacceptable response time standard.[18] A large portion of this delay is actually waiting for the consultations and approvals from NATO HQs before any forces can begin movement. In order for the deterrent to be credible, NATO must reinforce its commitment publically and conduct short notice training deployments of the VJTF that are initiated at the NATO HQs level.

NATO must update its graduated response plans and develop an executable defensive plan based on the force structure and geographic disposition in Europe. Instead of training solely on what the allies want to train on, NATO exercises must instead focus on integrating the specialized capabilities that allies have committed to providing to NATO. If the same capabilities exist in multiple countries, then NATO must exercise with all of them in order to ensure it has a trained resource at its disposal when needed. Political decisions from individual allies may influence what forces are available and when, and NATO's ability as an alliance should not hinge on one Alliance member's forces. A current example is bridging ability. If the Alliance operational plan requires the ability to bridge a river tactically, there are only a few allies that have that capability on the continent. The NATO exercises must work with all of them to ensure that they are ready and available in the event they are needed.

ACHIEVING STABILITY THROUGH RESILIENCE

As discussed in Chapter 1, the most likely course of action for Russia to pursue includes the technique of inciting a Russian minority in a former Warsaw Pact or near abroad country as a pretext for Russian involvement.[19] Russia could employ various ambiguous warfare techniques to generate confusion, spur a request for Russian assistance, or deliberately cause a state to fail—allowing for a Russian-friendly government to take over. Such ambiguous actions would be difficult to attribute to Russia, and would likely capitalize on the struggle within NATO to build a consensus for an immediate response. NATO considers civil unrest and most other ambiguous operations, such as cyberattacks, as internal security issues, which should be dealt with as a national responsibility under Article 3 of the North Atlantic Treaty.[20] If there was clear, factual evidence of Russian sponsorship of an ambiguous attack into a NATO country, the Alliance might

131

consider action under Article 5 of the North Atlantic Treaty, but such clear attribution is unlikely. If Russian actions in Ukraine and Crimea are any indicator, the ambiguous attacks will remain unattributed until Russian actions become a fait accompli and hence significantly more difficult to undo.

The key to countering this type of action is to ensure the allies in the border states have the ability to generate their own stability using internal tools to anticipate and react to ambiguous attacks.[21] This includes capabilities such as cyber defense, the ability to competently deal with civil unrest, and the ability to adequately deal with covert special operations disguised as terrorism. In most NATO countries, the responsibility to deal with these types of attacks does not rest solely with the military. It also resides with law enforcement, intelligence agencies, and the civil sector. Accordingly, any efforts to defend against such attacks must account for preparing all the various national entities and not just the militaries.

FOREIGN INTERNAL DEFENSE (FID): ENABLING RESILIENCE

> Foreign internal defense (FID) is the participation by civilian and military agencies of a government in any of the action programs taken by another government or other designated organization, to free and protect its society from subversion, lawlessness, insurgency, terrorism, and other threats to their security.[22]

In addition to strengthening external defense capabilities and capacity, the U.S. military also plays a critical security cooperation role in building the internal defense capabilities and capacities of allies and partners. Although it is most frequently associated with special operations forces (SOF) and is, in fact, a core SOF mission, FID can actually be a whole of government effort toward assisting another country to maintain security within its borders. Typically, U.S. forces engaged in FID activities have focused on counterinsurgency, counterterrorism, and counterdrug objectives. However, given the potential for Russia to engage in ambiguous operations, FID can play a critical role in building resilience and other capabilities among U.S. allies in Europe. By doctrine, FID is a subtask under the TSC umbrella. Many TSC efforts help to develop "dual-use" skills that the countries receiving the training can use in support of NATO operations outside of their borders or during internal strife if national laws allow.

Source: U.S. Army photo by SPC Timothy Clegg, *https://www.facebook.com/SOCEUR/photos/*.

U.S. and Estonian SOF conduct route planning for a ground infiltration during Exercise Spring Storm 2014. FID plays a critical role in theater security cooperation.

Figure 4-4. Foreign Internal Defense.

Although the United States TSC efforts are facilitating many of the military-focused assurance and deterrence tasks NATO has recently undertaken, there is room for improvement in gaining U.S. interagency support for conducting FID training. The goal for this type of FID would be to assist with strengthening the resilience of a NATO ally to ensure they are less vulnerable to Russian ambiguous actions. The challenge for conducting what might be thought of as "interagency FID" would be establishing priority countries, identifying focus areas, and getting the appropriate trainers in place. The key in every case is for the United States and allied or partner countries to jointly determine the lines of effort necessary to achieve specific and attainable objectives while considering NATO defense planning process priorities. The United States must be cognizant of the strategic end states for each Theater Campaign Plan (TCP) and associated country-specific Security Cooperation Sections, which should lay out the end states and the ways to achieve them, and should be coordinated with the U.S. Embassy Integrated Country Strategy and associated foreign assistance plans.

There are several challenges to employing an interagency FID effort to build resilience among NATO allies. First, the U.S. Department of State (DoS) and EUCOM must ensure that the DoS Regional Strategies and EUCOM's TCP are mutually supporting. There is no clear chain of command in this process, and it will certainly involve intense personal engagement from leaders across the interagency. The primary stakeholders, DoS and EUCOM, operate differently with respect to generating strategy. The presidentially appointed ambassadors are the lead for developing their country plans, which are then forwarded to the DoS in Washington for inclusion in the regional strategies. In the DoD, the policy offices of the Office of the Under Secretary of Defense for Policy (OUSDP) and EUCOM generate the strategy and then push it down to subordinate elements for execution. The common ground for decision-makers can be hard to determine since the Ambassador is the lead for DoS and is country-focused and the EUCOM commander is the lead for DoD and is regionally focused. Achieving unity of effort toward building resilient partners will require a constant, integrated engagement from both bureaucracies. Additionally, it would be invaluable to generate some form of interagency resilience strategy that would synchronize efforts.[23]

Another challenge will be getting the right inter-agency trainers in the right country at the right time. With no overall decision-maker across the interagency other than the President, organizations will have to choose to contribute to the effort versus being compelled to contribute. In a resource-constrained environment, the ability of agencies to surge people forward will remain difficult. A potential DoD contribution in this area would be to leverage the unique capabilities and relationships that exist in the National Guard State Partnership Program (SPP). Although it would not be a systemic fix, the National Guard frequently has citizen soldiers who have unique skills from their civilian life that would transfer over to assisting with FID efforts. Stereotypically, there are a high number of police officers in the Guard who would have the ability to train in civil disturbance response. Information technology professionals would also be invaluable assets in assisting the Allies with hardening their networks against Russian cyberattacks. Additional funding and authorities would be required to effectively pursue this course of action but, in the short term, the National Guard could assist with filling this gap. The relationships already built through years of the SPP would serve to enhance this type of training.

Source: U.S. Army photo by Kenneth C. Upsall, *https://www.flickr.com/photos/usarmyeurope_images*.

Latvian Chief of Defense Lieutenant General Raimonds Graube (left) and U.S. Chief of National Guard Bureau, and member of the Joint Chiefs of Staff, General Frank J. Grass discuss tasks associated with Operation ATLANTIC RESOLVE with U.S. Army Major Douglas A. Laxson and Lieutenant Colonel Felix A. Perez of the 2nd Battalion, 8th Calvary Regiment, 1st Brigade Combat Team, 1st Calvary Division at Adazi Training Area, Latvia on Nov. 7, 2014. The National Guard, through its SPP, plays a critical role in helping NATO allies enhance capabilities.

Figure 4-5. The Role of the National Guard.

The United States must also take into account the nature of the threat and the operational environment facing each ally when it considers training and equipping efforts. Each ally will use their forces in a manner informed by culture, history, geopolitics, and other factors, which ideally should shape the scope and breadth of U.S. efforts. For example, FID activities could enable the Baltic States in their efforts to counter ambiguous threats ultimately emanating from Moscow, but U.S. planners must be cognizant of Baltic State sensitivities toward their Russian-speaking populations. A large amount of the recommended FID training is already taking place under EUCOM's TSC efforts. What is currently lacking is a synchronized interagency effort that is focused on building national resiliency as a component of an overall country-specific strategy.

CLOSING THE GAPS

There are also several steps EUCOM can take to better focus its TSC efforts. First, EUCOM should re-examine its TSC processes. An efficient process should more effectively nest TSC efforts between EUCOM and USAREUR to ensure that USAREUR is focused on the right allies and capabilities. The United States needs to become more effective in Europe with streamlined TSC efforts between EUCOM and USAREUR improving the training level of individual allies, while best aligning the exercise program to support further development and demonstration of NATO capability.

Second, EUCOM should reduce the number of exercises in order to focus on high-quality, fully integrated NATO operations. The current pace and volume of exercises in EUCOM is generating a large amount of activity and has served its purpose in re-assuring the allies of the U.S. commitment to NATO. This activity is also likely having a deterrent effect on Russian intentions. However, a more focused exercise program that actually rehearses likely employment scenarios for NATO forces would have an even greater deterrent effect. By doing fewer exercises, with more resourcing and participation, EUCOM will more efficiently enable the Alliance. EUCOM should use the Joint Exercise Program to force multinational integration and encourage NATO command structure participation. An exercise that does not fully integrate the current and upcoming NATO command and control nodes misses the opportunity to rehearse a critical component of possible future operations. By rehearsing them, NATO can generate a deterrent effect against the very action they are designed to counter.

Third, EUCOM should improve public affairs and IO to ensure the United States is delivering the intended message. The current messaging in Europe focuses on reassurance and is focused primarily on a European audience. This emphasis on how busy the United States is in Europe and on how the Alliance is training offensive capabilities may be sending an unintended message to the Russians. NATO exercises should remain primarily defensive in nature and U.S. messaging should reinforce that the purpose of all training and exercises is to better prepare the Alliance to defend itself against Russian aggression. Russian IO will likely continue to promote the narrative that the Alliance is interested in attacking. However, a coherent U.S. public and IO campaign will minimize its impacts. Russian observers should be invited to attend all exercises to watch the defensive focus and leader engagement from senior U.S. officials should communicate the defensive message.

CONCLUSION

As part of the U.S. Army War College Project 1704 — an in-depth study of Russian Strategy in Eastern Europe — the study team recommended that NATO work to regain the initiative in Europe. A key pillar of this effort to regain the initiative was to, "Maintain credible land forces in theater."[24] The study recommended that to do this, NATO must "build and maintain a credible and scalable deterrent."[25] To establish the credible minimal deterrence, the study realized that landpower capability, both forward staged and rotational, would be critical.

The Russians must believe that NATO is capable of responding with overwhelming force, and indeed NATO must be capable of doing so, whether or not it is ever actually required. Although focused TSC is not a panacea, nor a perfect substitute for large-scale forward presence, in the current fiscal and political environment, it is a primary mechanism to shape exercises, capabilities, and operations to achieve a credible and capable deterrent effect.

ENDNOTES - CHAPTER 4

1. GEN Philip M. Breedlove, *United States European Command Theater Strategy*, United States European Command (EUCOM), Headquarters, October 2015, p. 4, available from *www.eucom.mil/*, accessed February 6, 2016.

2. Analogy derived from research discussions with a North Atlantic Treaty Organization (NATO) Staff Officer at the Supreme Headquarters Allied Powers Europe (SHAPE) Headquarters, November 4, 2015.

3. Joint Publication 3-0 defines theater security cooperation (TSC) as:

> Security cooperation involves all [DoD] interactions with foreign defense and security establishments to build defense relationships that promote specific U.S. security interests, develop allied and friendly military and security capabilities for internal and external defense for and multinational operations, and provide U.S. forces with peacetime and contingency access to the host nation.

United States Joint Chiefs of Staff, *Joint Operations*, Joint Publication 3-0, Washington, DC: United States Joint Chiefs of Staff, August 11, 2011, p. V-9.

4. Chuck Hagel, *Guidance for The Employment of the Force (GEF)*, U.S. Secretary of Defense Memorandum, February 2015, p. 32. Note: This extract from the GEF comes from an unclassified section of the document.

5. David A. Shlapak and Michael W. Johnson, *Reinforcing Deterrence on NATO's Eastern Flank: Wargaming the Defense of the Baltics*, Santa Monica, CA: RAND, 2016, p. 1, available from *www.rand.org/content/dam/rand/pubs/research_reports/RR1200/RR1253/RAND_RR1253.pdf*, accessed February 3, 2016.

6. Julie Ioffe, "Exclusive: The Pentagon Is Preparing New War Plans for a Baltic Battle Against Russia" *Foreign Policy*, September 18, 2015, available from *foreignpolicy.com.usawc.idm.oclc.org/2015/09/18/exclusive-the-pentagon-is-preparing-new-war-plans-for-a-baltic-battle-against-russia/*, accessed January 3, 2016."

7. Derived from discussions with LTC Reed Anderson, author of Chapter 2 of this monograph.

8. Benjamin Hodges, "Strong Europe" Lecture at the U.S. Army War College, Carlisle Barracks, PA, September 21, 2015.

9. Hagel.

10. Information derived from research discussions with NATO International Staff for Policy member on November 3, 2015.

11. Hagel.

12. Information derived from research discussions with NATO International Staff for Policy member on November 3, 2015.

13. Analogy derived from research discussions with U.S. Army Europe (USAREUR) Staffers on November 4, 2015.

14. Michael Hartmayer and John Hansen, "Security Cooperation in Support of Theater Strategy," *Military Review*, January-February 2013, p. 27.

15. Breedlove, p. 4.

16. Elbridge Colby and Jonathan Solomon, "Facing Russia: Conventional Defence and Deterrence in Europe," *Survival*, Vol. 56, Iss. 6, November 2015, p. 40, *www-tandfonline-com.usawc.idm. oclc.org/doi/abs/10.1080/00396338.2015.1116146*, accessed November 30, 2015.

17. Information derived from research discussions with USAREUR staff officers conducted by the author on January 14, 2016.

18. Information derived from research discussions with senior NATO/SHAPE members conducted by the author on November 3-4, 2015.

19. Colby and Solomon, p. 23.

20. Information derived from research discussions with Special Operations Command Europe (SOCEUR) staffers conducted by the author on November 4, 2015.

21. Franklin D. Kramer *et al.*, *NATO's New Strategy: Stability Generation*, Washington, DC: The Atlantic Council, 2015, available from *www.atlanticcouncil.org/publications/reports/nato-s-new-strate gy-stability-generation*, accessed April 14, 2016.

22. United States Joint Chiefs of Staff, *Foreign Internal Defense*, Joint Publication 3-22, Washington, DC: United States Joint Chiefs of Staff, July 12, 2010, p. ix.

23. Information derived from research discussions with Department of State staff members on February 23, 2016.

24. Doug Mastriano *et al.*, *Project 1704: A United States Army War College Analysis of Russian Strategy in Eastern Europe, and Appropriate U.S. Response and the Implications for U.S. Landpower*, Carlisle Barracks, PA: United States Army War College, 2015, p. 95.

25. *Ibid.*

CHAPTER 5

THE INFORMATION ENVIRONMENT:
A CRITICAL ELEMENT OFTEN NEGLECTED

In light of the new strategic environment in Europe, this monograph has addressed several ways to improve deterrence, including modifying U.S. Army posture in Europe. However, senior leaders should also consider the policies and activities required to help anticipate and counter Russia's adversarial moves while minimizing potential risks with the proposals laid out in this monograph. Most importantly, senior leaders have to consider how they communicate these policies to various audiences and how these activities are perceived.

This chapter will first assess how Russia manipulates information to achieve its goals. Next, the chapter will provide an overview of key Department of Defense (DoD) information and influence related resources, highlighting how critical it is for the United States and the North Atlantic Treaty Organization (NATO) to gain an advantage in Europe's highly contested information environment. Finally, any information campaign must also take into account that there is always the possibility that miscalculations by either side could occur, which could have disastrous consequences, and planners must therefore clearly understand and manage associated risks.

By dedicating additional resources and improving the coordination of efforts to inform and influence, the U.S. Army can reinforce its commitment to security in Europe and clearly communicate U.S. intentions to all audiences. Such a step is key to mitigating risk and addressing Russia's belligerence.

RUSSIA'S MANIPULATION OF THE
INFORMATION ENVIRONMENT

It is not unusual for highly centralized or authoritarian regimes to encourage and exploit a degree of paranoia, vis-à-vis foreign threats, to justify domestic control. Historically, Moscow has proven particularly adept at this, employing a robust and tightly controlled domestic information campaign. Russian President Vladimir Putin carries on this tradition of carefully shaping public perception, using fear of foreign aggression, as well as a call for returning Russia to its Cold War-era power status, to support a foreign policy that keeps the nation safe while simultaneously maintaining his "strong and stable" control of the government. Under Putin's leadership, Russia's foreign policy conveys the need to defeat aggression outside its borders. As stated on the official website of the Russian Mission to the European Union (EU):

> Russia is well placed to consolidate its role as one of the centres of the new multipolar system and actively impact the global situation with a view to ameliorating it, strengthening security and stability, putting in place favourable external conditions for the country's internal development to ensure sustainable economic growth and thus a higher quality of life for Russian citizens.[1]

Its incursion into Ukraine is an example of this policy, as it reflects how Russia said it would ensure domestic security for its citizens and affect the international order to obtain or safeguard its interests.

Not only does Putin's government shape the domestic perception of security as one that justifies military action to the Russian people, he has likewise manipulated the perception of Russian military action among various Western audiences. Following the revolution that occurred on February 22, 2014 that ousted then-Ukrainian President Victor Yanukovich, unidentified ground forces took control of eastern parts of Ukraine and the Crimean Peninsula. These troops wore military uniforms with no identifying insignia and balaclavas covering their faces, but were equipped with the same weaponry as Russian Special Forces. It is now clear that Russian-backed militant separatists and "other militant forces" in eastern Ukraine and Crimea fought to secure territory favorable to Russian interests and its foreign policy. However, Putin publicly denied that Russia had deployed troops into Ukraine and the ensuing confusion as to who the soldiers were caused a moment of hesitation among European leadership. As the former Supreme Allied Commander Europe (SACEUR), retired U.S. Army General Wesley Clark observed, "the evidence is right in front of your face but we couldn't bring ourselves to admit it because we didn't want to admit the implications of direct Russian aggression."[2]

The Russian narrative, supported by its actions, also sent a message to NATO and the EU concerning their ambitions for further expansion, or inclusion of Russia's near abroad into what Moscow perceives as a European sphere of influence. Russia has historically maintained influence over Ukraine. In Russia's view, a pro-Western Ukraine could eventually join NATO, much like the Baltic States did. Weakening the Alliance supports Russia's foreign policy of "putting in place favourable external conditions."[3] A fractured NATO would also serve to boost Putin's popularity as having stood up to additional NATO expansion, reinforced by the negative perception many Russians have developed toward the Alliance.[4] Putin's government continues to fuel the "fear of encroachment" rhetoric among Russians and it has promoted the idea of Russian humiliation "based on revisionist history."[5] Vladimir Putin has pointed out NATO's expansion as an affront to Russian honor as NATO granted membership to newly independent nations on Russia's borders.[6]

Putin's Internal Control of the Narrative.

With a firm grip on domestic media outlets, Putin's government has not only used fear of foreign encroachment to solidify his government's position and power, but it has also ignited Russian nationalism. With very high public approval ratings, Putin has been free to carry out foreign policy as he and his military see fit.[7] Putin's interests are very clear in a foreign policy where control of the near abroad is linked directly to domestic control and the *vertikal vlasti* discussed in the opening chapter of this monograph. Through careful manipulation of information to domestic audiences, Putin's government has influenced the national motivations of fear and honor to support Russia's foreign policy goals.

The Russian media has a long history of state control and it only experienced the relaxed environment of free and independent journalism immediately following the collapse of the Soviet Union. Soon after, oligarchs began to influence the media landscape, in some cases purchasing favorable coverage. By the end of the 1990s, the media was once again under heavy state control. Nataliya Rostova, a visiting scholar at the University of California Berkeley's Graduate School of Journalism, believes that since free press was "given from above," there was little concern when it was slowly taken away since the people "didn't really fight for it."[8] Her commentary highlights how there was little time for a free media to grow and mature and serves as an example of how Russians accept the government's control of media outlets using a methodology that is underhanded and effective.

One example of such cunning occurred in October 2015, during the start of Russia's aerial bombing in Syria. A weather forecaster on a state-owned television channel cheerfully told viewers, "Syria's weather was ideal for carrying out operational sorties." With a straight face, she continued with a lengthy analysis of weather conditions for bombing.[9] Another recent example in the online edition of *The Moscow Times*, an unnamed author accused the United States and its allies of waging a "hybrid war (economic, political, and-informational) against Russia for two decades" based on an alleged "'top' Russian investigator's findings."[10]

Thus, in this state-controlled media environment, Putin employs news outlets to legitimize Russian action in Syria and the centuries-old method of exploiting fear of subjugation and even invasion. In essence, Putin can shape and then leverage a Russian worldview, with historical resonance, where Europeans are encroaching from the west, Mongols are conducting a cyber-invasion from the east, and extremist Islamic terrorists are attacking from the south. As noted above though, Putin's information campaign is not limited to the domestic audience.

Using the same techniques, Russia spins news stories through outlets, including in Western Europe, to highlight decadence and corruption in the West as well as exploiting European security concerns, for example over the immigrant surge from the Middle East.[11] As noted in Chapter 1, the Russian strategy includes buying news outlets in Western Europe. Additionally, many parliamentarians in European governments have received financial support from bank and business institutions based in Russia or that are Russian-owned. These politicians can advance their positions and influence using the same Western media outlets that provide the Kremlin's worldview to a wide audience. As one NATO officer pointed out, what good is a robust defense of a nation when that nation's leadership hands over the keys to the kingdom?[12]

U.S. EFFORTS TO INFORM AND INFLUENCE

To address Putin's robust information campaign, the United States must continue to challenge Russia's misinformation. The Russian news outlet, RT (formerly Russia Today) "has an annual budget comparable in size to the BBC's World News Service,"[13] That amount in 2015 was roughly $361 million.[14] In comparison, the Department of State (DoS) requested $770,000 in the President's fiscal year 2017 budget for Voice of America and Radio Free Europe/Radio Liberty programming.[15]

DoD information-related capabilities are in a position to support these state-led activities, but DoD needs to resource and organize its own strategic communication efforts more effectively in theater. The President's fiscal year 2016 budget for the European Reassurance Initiative (ERI) references activities to counter malignant influence in Central and Eastern Europe in the defense-wide spending section and allocates $24 million "to increase partnership activities." This line item funds:

[Special Operations Force's] SOF persistent presence [activities] to train, advise, and assist Allies and conduct defense planning with select countries to counter malign influence in Central and Eastern Europe.[16]

The President's fiscal year 2017 budget request adds an additional $8 million for the U.S. European Command (EUCOM) to monitor the information environment, $5 million for establishment of a U.S. Army influence platform, and $43.5 million for SOF presence and partnership activities that also include activities to counter malignant influence in Central and Eastern Europe.[17] This budget request amount is an increase to previous funding to counter propaganda and misinformation but it also shows disconnect across the DoD's capabilities and effort in Europe to conduct effective information operations.

The bulk of U.S. Special Operations Command (SOCOM) military information support operations (MISO) or (psychological operations [PSYOPS] in NATO) efforts are still focused on and funded to counter violent extremist ideology, predominantly from the Middle East. The SOCOM MISO endeavors are increasingly coordinated with the DoS's new Global Engagement Center, led by a former Assistant Secretary of Defense for Special Operations and Low Intensity Conflict. However, its official charter is heavily anti-Islamic State of Iraq and the Levant (ISIL) (also known as the Islamic State in Iraq and Syria [ISIS] or Daesh) focused.[18] In fact, funding for MISO programs in Europe is at a level lower than the resources allocated to the Middle East and Africa.

In addition to financial resourcing, success in planning and executing these programs requires professionals dedicated to the task. Current Army doctrine describes, "inform and influence activities" replacing information operations (IO), which covered a wider scope of activities such as electronic warfare and computer network operations. Over a decade of Army operations have seen public affairs professionals conduct the informing, while MISO officers and noncommissioned officers (NCOs) carry out influence and military deception tasks.

Within the U.S. Army, a dedicated officer-only IO career field, trained to only integrate but not to conduct MISO or public affairs, is responsible for coordinating EUCOM's limited resources to counter Putin's information campaign. Specifically, as of October 2016 there will be a handful of IO officer authorizations in EUCOM—a colonel and a lieutenant colonel at EUCOM headquarters (HQ), a lieutenant colonel at Special Operations Command Europe (SOCEUR), a lieutenant colonel and two majors at U.S. Army Europe (USAREUR), and a lieutenant colonel and major at 7th Army. At the same time, the highest-ranking MISO planner on the EUCOM staff will be a staff sergeant while a major and captain will be authorized for SOCEUR. The USAREUR HQ will have no authorizations for MISO planners. Currently, its chief IO staff officer is a civil affairs colonel. Only its subordinate 7th Army HQ staff is authorized a MISO major and a sergeant major.[19]

While, MISO is a SOF function, the bulk of MISO capability dedicated to supporting conventional forces resides in the U.S. Army Reserve and is not directly connected to or under the command of the Army's SOF training and doctrinal institutions. There is only one active component MISO battalion (about 250 personnel), coordinating its activities through SOCEUR, and occasional reserve component support dedicated to the European theater. A dedicated public affairs career branch also coordinates its communication activities with both IO planners as well as MISO staff sections. However, to operate in this highly contested information environment and be successful in countering Russian propaganda, the U.S. Army requires dedicated inform and influence planners in Europe to match the increased ERI funding.

Furthermore, the purpose and structure of the Army's information-related capabilities are decentralized, yet the authorities and approvals for information programs and products are highly centralized. The decentralized nature of various information-related staff structures resulted in the creation of a career field of coordinators untrained in the capabilities they are charged to integrate—this is akin to creating a combat operations coordination career field in which none of the personnel in that specialty have previously served or received training as combat arms officers. The tendency in the Army over the last decade is for influence program and product approvals to reside at a very senior (major general or lieutenant general) officer level. It would be far more effective and efficient to push approval authority for execution to lower levels of command.

Additionally, to inform European audiences, Army public affairs efforts must continue to highlight bilateral and multilateral events to reassure allies and partners that the Alliance is unshakeable and that the United States remains committed to European security. Army public affairs officers and their activities should also publicize joint exercises that highlight distinct capabilities that can deter aggressive behavior toward NATO and Europe, and must clearly highlight to Russian leaders the defensive nature of these joint exercises. Most importantly, as mentioned in an earlier chapter, strategic communication in support of reassurance to European audiences must be NATO-centric. European populations may be less concerned with the United States' capability to "come to their rescue" and instead, need to know what other NATO member militaries are doing to deter Russia.[20] Influence activities need to focus on countering Russia's anti-Europe propaganda and developing the same military deception capabilities that are a hallmark of Russia's ambiguous warfare. The success of U.S. programs requires more trained inform and influence professionals who can be trusted to approve and execute plans to counter Russian disinformation rapidly. Fundamentally, U.S. military inform and influence structures must be consolidated in capability and purpose and decentralized in approval and execution.[21]

Inform and influence activity in Europe should be clearly coordinated with other U.S. Government strategic communications efforts, particularly those coordinated out of U.S. embassies in Europe and Eurasia, as well as those of European Allies and partners. In a similar fashion to the DoS's counter-ISIL focused Global Engagement Center, the U.S. Army with NATO, along with the DoS public diplomacy efforts, should regularly share and coordinate efforts to take advantage of flaws in the Russian narrative. Non-military media outlets such as Radio Free Europe excel at fostering and maintaining relationships with free press and media agencies throughout the world. A recent survey conducted in the Baltic States on the consumption and influence of Russian-language media found that of domestic, Russian-backed, and international news sources, Russian speakers in all three Baltic States ranked "Kremlin-backed media as the least trustworthy."[22]

These perceptions represent an opportunity to provide information supporting a Western European and NATO narrative. More importantly, fostering relationships helps media outlets to enhance transparency and disclose "the identities of [Russian] government-sponsored backers of European political parties and how they are financed."[23] The advantage for U.S. and NATO strategic communication endeavors is having free and independent media outlets reporting reliable information to European audiences. This construct provides more than one voice or source of information in order for populations to arrive at a conclusion that aligns with the free and democratic values that the United States and NATO allies espouse and defend. Exposing Russian-backed media across print, television, radio, and the Internet to create transparency and show how all of its information is carefully manipulated by one source weakens the effectiveness of the Russian Government's propaganda operations.

MITIGATING RISK TO AN INFORMATION CAMPAIGN

Previous chapters recommend the robust application of inform and influence activities to support NATO deterrence. However, there is risk to U.S. and NATO credibility if bold rhetoric directed at the Russian Government does not come with the necessary military resources that are needed to promote deterrence. Positive steps to reinforce deterrence include the requested fourfold increase to the ERI budget and the heel-to-toe rotation of an armored brigade in Europe.[24]

Therein lies another risk: NATO and U.S. information efforts could reinforce Putin's domestic fear mongering that NATO's publicized military maneuvers are a sign of preparations for a future invasion of the Russian homeland. Mitigating the risk of miscalculating by the Russian military will require very clear communication to Russian leaders that all of NATO's activities are defensive in nature, lest both sides fall into a misperception leading to a security dilemma, or worse, open conflict.

Another risk of "too much" reassurance to European allies is the development of an over reliance on the United States to perform the greater part of conventional deterrence in Europe. Therefore, U.S. information efforts in Europe need to support the focused security cooperation recommendations made in Chapter 4, and these efforts should support U.S. diplomacy to prompt NATO members to develop their own military deterrence capabilities.

Additionally, the two deterrence strategies discussed in Chapter 2 require an effective information campaign to mitigate the risks associated with them. The first strategy, deterrence by denial, has two parts: denying an adversary access through presence, and denying an adversary the ability to fracture and influence the Alliance. The first part requires the presence of NATO member military units in areas that Russia seeks to control, such as the Baltic States. There is risk associated with NATO units operating in areas with large numbers of ethnic Russians, which Moscow continues to consider its citizens. However, many of these Russian-speaking enclaves already do not trust Kremlin-based news sources, as discussed earlier, thus presenting an opportunity in winning popular support for a NATO presence even among Russian-speaking minorities.

There is further risk associated with having the forces either permanently stationed or present on a rotational basis in these areas. The U.S. Army War College's Project 1704 called for stationing "NATO (especially U.S.) forces in the Baltic countries" as the best means of deterring Russia.[25] While such an approach may present an effective deterrence, it does so at the risk of escalating a Russian military response along the border and providing propaganda fodder for Russian news media to highlight the "alarming presence" of significant NATO forces on those borders. To mitigate this risk requires substantial NATO-member media engagement to communicate the defensive nature of Alliance forces, a continued emphasis on rotational deployments (vice permanent basing) from across NATO, and the use of capability-developing exercises for visiting units.

The other part of the deterrence by denial strategy is impeding Putin's ability to fracture and influence the Alliance. Chapter 2 focuses on the substantial U.S. DoD, interagency, and bilateral interaction necessary for NATO members to develop resilient law enforcement and security institutions. Alliance efforts must also include coordination with media outlets, especially those throughout North America and Europe that foster free and independent journalism. This will help to provide the transparency that undermines Russia's media influence and disinformation campaigns in Europe. NATO must also seek to elicit the support of nongovernmental organizations dedicated to fostering democratic ideals and reducing political corruption. Doing too little on these fronts creates opportunities for Russia to move in with large amounts of cash to bribe and buy influence in the media and in European governments.

The second deterrence strategy is deterrence by punishment, in which NATO uses military force to damage or destroy overt Russian military aggression toward a NATO member. As addressed in previous chapters, there is much the Alliance needs to do to develop the necessary capabilities, and this requires a commitment to providing the requisite resources, without which the Alliance and the United States risk being unable to provide effective deterrence. The request for increased ERI funding should help, but it also requires a concerted communications effort by the United States to NATO allies, highlighting combined exercises and training, designed to show the benefit of investing in rapid response forces that demonstrate a credible deterrence capability.

Another key capability to mitigate risk in this deterrence strategy is to continue SOF training with NATO allies focusing on unconventional warfare as well as IO. U.S. Army Special Forces based in Germany still coordinate several joint training exercises every year. A Russian attack against the three Baltic States may occur swiftly but the costs associated with an invasion and its subsequent occupation may be prohibitive, especially if Putin realizes he may lose the information war. A well-trained and capable force, conventional or otherwise, which is capable of IO and military deception as part of a broader, prolonged insurgency may actually increase the deterrent effect.

CONCLUSION

Seizing the initiative for the information campaign to counter Russian aggression and actions is not simple. Moscow's *vertikal vlasti* gives Russia an advantage that open and free societies do not have. However, that does not preclude the United States, NATO, and individual European allies from working together to develop a well-considered information campaign that is capable of countering Russian information. It should also serve to mitigate the risks associated with U.S. and NATO activities designed to enhance the Alliance's ability to defend itself and deter Russian aggression on or aimed at Alliance territory.

As discussed, in order to effectively develop and implement such an effort, the DoD and its interagency partners need to make several changes, without which Russia will retain the initiative. First, the Joint Staff, in coordination with the services, should reconsider manning levels of appropriate staff expertise to plan and manage information campaigns at EUCOM, USAREUR, and within the proposed two-star HQ addressed in Chapter 3. These staff experts at the combatant command (CCMD) level should have all necessary authorities for planning and implementation, and should synchronize efforts with the regional desk officers within EUCOM's Planning Directorate, with EUCOM exercise planners, and with other relevant stakeholders. These stakeholders include subordinate units within EUCOM, especially SOCEUR, which retains a critical role in IO, as well as the U.S. Embassy country teams and the DoS's Global Engagement Center.

The DoD should also synchronize its information campaign with strategic objectives. While it continues efforts to counter extremist terrorist organizations in Europe, the DoD must also enhance information campaigns focused on Russia. This should not be done in a vacuum. Such efforts should include close coordination with U.S. country team efforts to ensure message synchronization. Further, both the DoD and

DoS should ensure they have effective mechanisms to measure the effect of their coordinated information campaigns, and make necessary adjustments as the information environment evolves. Capturing these elements in both the EUCOM Theater Campaign Plan (TCP) (to include the country-specific security cooperation sections) and the U.S. Embassy Integrated Country Strategy, is critical for codifying the approaches and providing baselines from which to make necessary adjustments.

There is not much the United States or NATO can do to change the way Russia uses information to achieve its security objectives. However, effectively targeting its own operations to counter Russian information activities—and doing so in a timely and proactive manner—can mitigate the effect of Russian efforts as well as the risks associated with U.S. and Alliance military activity in the Baltic States and Eastern Europe.

Sun Tzu stated, "Thus a victorious army wins its victories before seeking battle; an army destined to defeat fights in the hope of winning."[26] These words of the ancient strategist offer sound advice to military planners and policymakers in determining how best to posture U.S. Army forces in Europe. As noted in Chapter 4, the objective to seek victory without resorting to a costly and potentially catastrophic armed conflict should be considered a principal aim of current U.S. foreign policy.

ENDNOTES - CHAPTER 5

1. Permanent Mission of the Russian Federation to the European Union, Ministry of Foreign Affairs, "Russian Foreign Policy," available from *www.russianmission.eu/en/russian-foreign-policy*, accessed December 28, 2015.

2. General (Ret.) Wesley Clark, Interview originally aired February 18, 2015 on BBC News — Europe, The Inquiry, "How strong is the NATO military alliance?" available from *www.bbc.com/news/world-europe-31503859*, accessed September 30, 2015.

3. Permanent Mission of the Russian Federation.

4. Gordon Hahn, "It's Not 'Putin's Russia' - It's 'Russia's Putin'," Russia Insider, December 10, 2015, available from *russia-insider.com/en/politics/its-not-putins-russia-its-russias-putin/ri11772*, accessed April 27, 2016. This article refers to several surveys taken during the 1990s (by Russian language VTsIOM opinion survey) where Russians:

> felt to one degree or another that Russia had something to fear in countries joining NATO, only 31 percent did not think so. By June 1999, VTsIOM found that 73 percent of Russian citizens had a negative view of NATO, 27 percent – a positive view. This was particularly true regarding NATO expansion to former Soviet republics.

The author notes the change in survey questions regarding "fear" and "negative view of North Atlantic Treaty Organization (NATO)."

5. Anne Applebaum, "The Myth of Russian Humiliation," *The Washington Post*, October 17, 2014, available from *https://www.washingtonpost.com/opinions/anne-applebaum-nato-pays-a-heavy-price-for-giving-russia-too-much-credita-true-achievement-under-threat/2014/10/17/5b3a6f2a-5617-11e4-809b-8cc0a295c773_story.html*, accessed February 10, 2016.

6. See both Michael Rühle, "NATO enlargement and Russia: myths and realities," *NATO Review*, 2014, available from *www.nato.int/docu/review/2014/Russia-Ukraine-Nato-crisis/Nato-enlarge*

ment-Russia/EN/index.htm, accessed April 27, 2016; and John Pat Willerton, "Willerton on Tsygankov, 'Russia and the West from Alexander to Putin: Honor in International Relations'," book review of Andrei P. Tsygankov's, *Russia and the West from Alexander to Putin: Honor in International Relations*, East Lansing, MI: H-Diplo, Michigan State University, May 2013, available from *https://networks.h-net.org/node/28443/reviews/30483/willerton-tsygankov-russia-and-west-alexander-putin-honor-international*, accessed November 30, 2015.

7. Alberto Nardelli, Jennifer Rankin, and George Arnette, "Vladimir Putin's approval rating at record levels," *The Guardian*—U.S. Edition, July 23, 2015 available from *www.theguardian.com/world/datablog/2015/jul/23/vladimir-putins-approval-rating-at-record-levels*, accessed November 30, 2015.

8. Eline Gordts, "Putin's Press: How Russia's President Controls The News," *The World Post*, a partnership of *The Huffington Post* and Berggruen Institute, October 24, 2015, available from *www.huffingtonpost.com/entry/vladimir-putin-russia-news-media_us_56215944e4b0bce34700b1df*, accessed February 10, 2016.

9. Moscow AFP, "Russian TV forecasts 'good weather for bombing' in Syria," Yahoo! News, October 5, 2015, available from *news.yahoo.com/russian-tv-forecasts-good-weather-bombing-syria-131355437.html*, accessed February 10, 2016.

10. "Russia's Top Investigator Sees U.S. Hand in Economic Crisis, Litvinenko Probe," *The Moscow Times*, February 12, 2016, available from *www.themoscowtimes.com/news/article/russias-top-investigator-sees-us-hand-in-economic-crisis-litvinenko-probe/559315.html*, accessed February 13, 2016.

11. Heather A. Conley, "Putin's Europe," in Craig Cohan and Melissa G. Dalton eds., *2016 Global Forecast*, Washington, DC: Center for Strategic and International Studies, 2015, p. 38, available from *csis.org/files/publication/151116_Cohen_GlobalForecast2016_Web.pdf*, accessed November 28, 2015.

12. Analogy derived from a discussion with a Lithuanian Army officer in 2013 and also supported in Conley, p. 40, where she highlights how "Putin has perfected the art of 'managed

democracy' in Russia—where Russian authorities 'arrange both the elections and the results'—the Kremlin is now attempting to 'manage' several other European democracies."

13. Conley, p. 38.

14. Ashley Kirk, "BBC Charter Review: How does the BBC spend its money?" *The Telegraph,* July 16, 2015, available from *www.telegraph.co.uk/news/bbc/11744085/BBC-Charter-Review-How-does-the-BBC-spend-its-money.html*, accessed March 14, 2016.

15. The Secretary of State, "Congressional Budget Justification Department of State, Foreign Operations, and Related Programs," February 9, 2016, available from *www.state.gov/documents/organi zation/252179.pdf*, accessed March 14, 2016.

16. Office of the Under Secretary of Defense (Comptroller), "European Reassurance Initiative," Department of Defense Budget Fiscal Year (FY) 2016, Washington DC: Department of Defense, February 2015. p. 12.

17. Office of the Under Secretary of Defense (Comptroller), "European Reassurance Initiative," Department of Defense Budget Fiscal Year (FY) 2017, Washington DC: Department of Defense, February 2016.

18. U.S. Department of State, Office of the Spokesperson, "A New Center for Global Engagement," Fact Sheet, January 8, 2016, available from *www.state.gov/r/pa/prs/ps/2016/01/251066.htm*, accessed January 18, 2016.

19. Information derived from interviews between the authors and members of U.S. Army Human Resources Command, March 11, 2016.

20. Information derived from interviews between the authors and a member of the NATO International Staff for Policy, November 3, 2015.

21. Information derived from discussions with U.S. Army Europe (USAREUR), Special Operations Command Europe (SO-CEUR), U.S. Special Operations Command (USSOCOM), and U.S.

European Command (EUCOM) Information Operations (IO), Public Affairs Office (PAO), and military information support operations (MISO) staff members highlighting the Department of Defense's resourcing priority toward counter violent extremist ideology programs, sluggish program approvals due to high level approval authorities, and the disjointed nature of a non-MISO trained IO career field supporting conventional Army staff structures while active MISO personnel predominantly support Special Operations Force (SOF) unit headquarters (HQ).

22. Broadcasting Board of Governors, "Credibility of Russian Media Lacking in Baltic Nations," Press Release, February 9, 2016, Washington, DC, available from *www.bbg.gov/blog/2016/02/09/ credibility-of-russian-media-lacking-in-baltic-nations/*, accessed February 12, 2016.

23. Conley, p. 39.

24. Jen Judson, "US Army Budget to Build Force Size in Europe," *Defense News*, February 12, 2016, available from *www.de fensenews.com/story/defense/land/army/2016/02/09/us-army-budget-build-force-size-europe/80063172/*, accessed February 14, 2016.

25. Doug Mastriano *et al.*, *Project 1704: A United States Army War College Analysis of Russian Strategy in Eastern Europe, and Appropriate U.S. Response and the Implications for U.S. Landpower*, Carlisle Barracks, PA: United States Army War College, 2015, p. 9.

26. Sun Tzu, trans. by Samuel Griffith, *The Art of War*, New York: Oxford University Press, 1963, p. 87.

CHAPTER 6

CONCLUSIONS AND RECOMMENDATIONS

Over the last two decades, as hope ensued that the Cold War's end would create lasting peace and stability in Europe, the United States and North Atlantic Treaty Organization (NATO) drew down their forces and significantly reduced their force posture in Europe. In the last decade, Russia has increased its military, economic, and informational capabilities, and boldly employed them to pursue its objectives. These objectives have included increasing its influence in Europe, slowing the expansion of NATO and the European Union (EU), and creating fractures within Europe so that Russia could exert influence on its own terms.

Understanding Russian foreign policy aims and, more importantly, what drives Russian President Vladimir Putin's decision-making process is critical for influencing Russia. Even with increased understanding, tempering Russia's behavior will continue to present challenges. For this reason, the United States and its allies must address and be prepared to respond to Russian aggression, to include its use of both conventional forces and ambiguous warfare. The military element of Western power is critical here, but it should be used with particular care.

Given current capabilities, NATO is not able to prevent a Russian conventional attack into Alliance territory. This diminishes the Alliance's ability to deter Russia from using conventional or ambiguous threats to achieve its objectives to fracture the Alliance and gain influence in Europe. The military approach outlined in this monograph therefore includes the development of capabilities that provide the Alliance with the ability to not only respond to Russian aggression, but more importantly serve as a deterrent against such possible aggression. The consolidated effect of such efforts as outlined in this monograph should increase the perceived costs of Russian aggression and the probability of Moscow incurring such costs, and it should decrease the probability of Russia deriving benefits from its actions.

To develop such capabilities requires a concerted effort on the part of NATO, the EU, and their member states. For instance, European NATO members should continue searching for more effective ways to increase capabilities and progressively increase their defense budgets. U.S. European Command (EUCOM) and U.S. Army Europe (USAREUR) must more effectively align their security cooperation activities to support capability development, especially as identified through NATO's defense planning process. The United States and its allies must employ a coordinated, whole of government effort to address those capabilities that fall beyond the scope of the military, such as law enforcement. It is through such actions that the West can develop a capable force that underpins the credibility of its commitment to defend Alliance territory through deterrence.

More specifically, this monograph also identifies areas where the U.S. Army and NATO allies should focus efforts to achieve defined effects in response to Russian foreign policy. It does so fully recognizing that the United States has tried for many years to encourage its European NATO allies to pull a greater share of the burden. This monograph also recognizes that with global commitments, the United States can no longer afford to lift the bar from the allies when it becomes too heavy. Winning in a complex world indeed relies on allies, and the United States should help the allies succeed in pulling their share of the burden. With that in mind, and in the context of the entire monograph, this monograph identifies the following key considerations for senior leaders and then proposes a series of recommendations.

KEY CONSIDERATIONS

- The United States, and NATO, cannot afford to reassure allies to the point where they solely rely on the United States to ensure their security.
- Any policy or strategy toward Russia must understand Russian intentions and the likelihood of a conventional attack—balanced against the reality of potential ambiguous activities and Russian influence in Europe.
- The United States and NATO must be careful that its reassurance activities do not provoke further Russian aggression, or lead to a new security dilemma.

RECOMMENDATIONS

- The U.S. Army should assign, allocate, and apportion forces versus aligning them, in support of EUCOM's Theater Campaign Plan (TCP) and contingency plans.
- The U.S. Army should assign a Joint Task Force (JTF)-capable two-star headquarters (HQ) to USAREUR.
- The U.S. Army should establish a rotational allocation of an Armored Brigade Combat Team (ABCT) that provides a continuous armor presence in Europe.

RECOMMENDATIONS CONT.

- The U.S. Army should ensure units receive the requisite security cooperation, and/or foreign internal defense (FID)-specific training for conventional units.
- The National Guard's State Partnership Program should focus more explicitly on building and maintaining allies' resiliency in the face of ambiguous warfare.
- EUCOM should re-examine its theater security cooperation (TSC) process to nest efforts between EUCOM and USAREUR more effectively.
  - EUCOM and USAREUR should more effectively make use of NATO capability targets, part of the NATO Defense Planning Process, to define the types of activities that will focus on lacking capabilities.
  - EUCOM should reduce the number of exercises in order to focus on high-quality, fully integrated NATO operations.
  - EUCOM should synchronize country-specific sections of its Theater Campaign Plan with the U.S. Embassy Integrated Country Strategies.
- EUCOM and USAREUR should ensure staffs are trained, particularly those involved in security cooperation, to conduct strategic and operational planning, and to understand the nesting of national security objectives with Alliance capability targets.
- The Joint Staff and the U.S. Army should improve manning levels of appropriate staff expertise to plan and manage the "inform and influence" activities at EUCOM, subordinate units, and within the proposed two-star HQ.
- The Department of Defense (DoD) and Department of State (DoS) should ensure they have effective mechanisms to coordinate information campaigns, and make necessary adjustments as the information environment evolves.

RECOMMENDATIONS CONT.

- The DoD should reconsider its representation at the U.S. Mission to the EU to enhance its ability to synchronize efforts with NATO and EUCOM.
- Washington needs to build a concerted effort among interagency partners to identify areas where the United States can assist European NATO members develop capabilities to deter Russia's ambiguous warfare.
- NATO should re-examine The Supreme Allied Commander Europe's (SACEUR's) authority to reposition forces in Europe.
- NATO should move toward a NATO multinational logistics capability.
- NATO should streamline the timeline for approvals of counter-Russia actions.
- NATO should reinitiate dialogue with Russia.

By implementing the above recommendations, while remaining mindful of the key considerations, the West can more effectively and efficiently employ the military tools at its disposal to manage a resurgent Russia.

U.S. ARMY WAR COLLEGE

Major General William E. Rapp
Commandant

*****

STRATEGIC STUDIES INSTITUTE
and
U.S. ARMY WAR COLLEGE PRESS

Director
Professor Douglas C. Lovelace, Jr.

Director of Research
Dr. Steven K. Metz

Authors
Lieutenant Colonel R. Reed Anderson
Colonel Patrick J. Ellis
Lieutenant Colonel Antonio M. Paz
Lieutenant Colonel Kyle A. Reed
Lieutenant Colonel Lendy "Alamo" Renegar
Lieutenant Colonel John T. Vaughan

Editor for Production
Dr. James G. Pierce

Publications Assistant
Ms. Denise J. Kersting

*****

Composition
Mrs. Jennifer E. Nevil